D1616105

RETHINKING HOW WE THINK

Also by Charles Johnston:

The Creative Imperative: Human Growth and Planetary Evolution

Necessary Wisdom: Meeting the Challenge of a New Cultural Maturity

Pattern and Reality: A Brief Introduction to Creative Systems Theory

The Power of Diversity: An Introduction to the Creative Systems Personality Typology

An Evolutionary History of Music: Introducing Creative Systems Theory Through the Language of Sound (DVD)

Quick and Dirty Answers to the Biggest of Questions: Creative Systems Theory Explains What It Is All About (Really)

Cultural Maturity: A Guidebook for the Future

Hope and the Future: Confronting Today's Crisis of Purpose

On the Evolution of Intimacy: A Brief Exploration into the Past, Present, and Future of Gender and Love

Online:

The Institute for Creative Development: www.CreativeSystems.org

Creative Systems Theory: www.CSTHome.org

Cultural Maturity: www.CulturalMaturity.org

The Creative Systems Personality Typology: www.CSPTHome.org

An Evolutionary History of Music: www.Evolmusic.org

Cultural Maturity: A Blog for the Future: www.CulturalMaturityBlog.net

Looking To The Future podcast: www.LookingtotheFuture.net

RETHINKING
HOW WE THINK

Integrative Meta-Perspective
and the Cognitive
"Growing Up"
On Which Our Future Depends

CHARLES M. JOHNSTON MD

The Institute for Creative Development (ICD) Press
Seattle, Washington

Publisher's Cataloging-In-Publication Data
(Prepared by The Donohue Group, Inc.)

Johnston, Charles M.
    Rethinking how we think : integrative meta-perspective and the cognitive
    "growing up" on which our future depends / Charles M. Johnston MD.
Seattle, Washington : The Institute for Creative Development (ICD) Press, [2020] |
    Include bibliographical references and index.
    ISBN 9781732219045
    ISBN 9781732219083 (ebook)
1. LCSH: Thought and thinking. 2. Common sense. 3. Comprehension. 4. Future,
    The—Psychological aspects.
LCC BF441 .J64 2020 (print)
LCC BF441 (ebook)
DDC 153.42—dc23

The Institute for Creative Development (ICD) Press, Seattle, Washington

Copyright © 2020 by Charles M. Johnston, MD. All rights reserved. No part of this
book may be reproduced, except for reviews and brief excerpts with attribution, without the written permission of the publisher. Manufactured in the United States of
America. For information, address The Institute for Creative Development (ICD)
Press, 4324 Meridian Ave. N., Seattle, WA 98103, or ICDPressinfo@gmail.com.

Cover design by Warren Godfrey

Author photo by Brad Kevelin

Library of Congress Control Number: 2019907358 First printing 2020

RETHINKING HOW WE THINK

Setting the Conceptual Stage

My life's work as a psychiatrist and futurist has focused on making sense of the times we live in and addressing critical challenges ahead for us as a species. These efforts have included twenty years directing the Institute for Creative Development, a Seattle-based think tank and center for advanced leadership training and, in the many years that followed, writing books about what these essential challenges will require of us. This book addresses one of the most pivotal and ultimately critical insights from these efforts.

My time with the Institute provides an introductory glimpse. The Institute worked to identify the questions that would be most important for future human well-being and brought together the best minds to grapple with them. It also trained people in the leadership abilities needed to engage the challenges presented by these questions.

Over time, a striking recognition became forefront in our efforts. We saw that successfully addressing the most important future questions would require not just making better choices, but developing new kinds of skills and capacities. Much that we did centered around making sense of those new skills and capacities and their implications.

And there was an even more radical and foundational recognition. We saw that deeply understanding those new skills and capacities required thinking in new ways. By "new ways" I don't mean just being more inventive in one's conclusions. We saw that understanding and realizing needed new skills and capacities would require thinking in ways that are fundamentally new to our time.

This further recognition had striking consequences. Right off, it confronted us with how demanding what we were attempting to do would necessarily be. We had to face that our task would need to involve more than just teaching ideas and approaches. We would have to engage people in making a major leap in perspective. And we had to accept that very often conclusions we might reach would be ten, twenty, or thirty years ahead of what most people might easily grasp.

But we also saw that there was an important way that this further recognition could make what we were trying to accomplish simpler. If we could help people think in these new ways, the needed new skills and capacities would follow. We also found something else that came from the particular kind of newness these new ways of understanding represented. While for most people they would initially be a stretch—often a considerable stretch—with time they would come to seem almost obvious, like common sense.

This book is equally about the complexity of the challenges ahead for the species and the elegant simplicity of what engaging them effectively can involve.

My two recent books, *Hope and the Future: Confronting Today's Crisis of Purpose* and *Cultural Maturity: A Guidebook for the Future* focused primarily on those needed new skills and capacities.[1] *Rethinking How We Think* turns more directly to needed changes in how we understand, to the cognitive reordering on which our future increasingly depends. In doing so, it engages the question of what our times require of us as a species in a manner that is particularly spare and direct.

The specific way I will talk about this cognitive reordering has its roots in Creative Systems Theory (CST), a comprehensive framework for understanding purpose, change, and interrelationship in human systems developed by myself and colleagues at the Institute.[2] CST makes

---

1   *Hope and the Future* is an introductory book written for a general audience. *Cultural Maturity* is a comprehensive work written for leaders committed to developing needed new capacities.

2   I first presented Creative Systems Theory's general approach in 1984 with my book *The Creative Imperative*. In 1992, I wrote *Patterning and Reality* as a teaching resource to introduce people to the basic ideas of CST. The latest thinking on CST can be found on the Institute for Creative Development website (www.creativesystems.org). I am currently in the process of writing a major work that summarizes the thinking of CST

important contributions to cognitive science. It delineates how our cognitive mechanisms have worked in fundamentally different ways at different times in culture's story. It also delineates how these different kinds of cognitive organization produce predictably different kinds of values and worldviews.

For our task in these pages, a particular implication of this evolutionary picture has special significance. CST predicts that our times should be challenging us to take a critical further step in this progression beyond the kind of thinking that gave us the great achievements of our Modern Age. We will look at how the evidence supports this result. We will also see how this new chapter in our human development will be critical if we are to successfully advance as a species—indeed if we are just to have the decisions we make going forward not bring an end to the human experiment. CST calls this necessary "growing up" as a species Cultural Maturity.[3]

Most immediately, Cultural Maturity's changes challenge us to step beyond what has been in effect a parent/child relationship with our cultural contexts. We see the beginnings of such change today with how familiar cultural dictates such as traditional gender roles and clear moral codes are becoming less absolute. Our times are demanding that we take a critical new kind of responsibility not just for how we act, but also for how we understand.

More deeply, Cultural Maturity's changes produce a new kind of cognitive organization. It is this that makes new skills and capacities possible. It is also what allows us to think in more complex and nuanced ways. CST uses the term Integrative Meta-perspective to describe this new kind of cognitive organization. While the term is a bit of a mouthful, I've come to deeply appreciate it—and use it often. It quite precisely describes the needed changes.

Integrative Meta-perspective will here have a dual role. It will provide the topic for our inquiry. I will argue that any kind of future we

---

and how it has evolved over the course of my life.

3 I put the phrase "growing up" in quotes because, as we will see, its reference is to a particular kind of maturation—not to what we find with first becoming an adult, but rather to the changes that occur as a person addresses the developmental tasks of life's second half.

would want to live in will require that we learn to think in the more mature and complete ways that Integrative Meta-perspective makes possible. It will also give us the needed lens for understanding. These reflections will make little sense without at least a beginning capacity for Integrative Meta-perspective.

Over the course of the book, I will describe multiple ways in which Integrative Meta-perspective alters understanding, but one will have particular importance. Integrative Meta-perspective produces thinking that is more specifically "systemic." And more than this, by taking us beyond more familiar engineering sorts of systemic thinking, it produces a kind of systemic understanding that is itself new. Integrative Meta-perspective offers that we might more directly address the deeper kind of systemic complexity that orders life, and, more specifically, the particular kind of systemic complexity that makes us human. We will look at how this additional step is critical to understanding that can serve us going forward.

I will often draw on a simple image to represent the needed new kind of systemic understanding: a box of crayons with its multiple hues. The various crayons represent various systemic aspects. And the box represents the ability to get our minds around a larger systemic picture. We will see how the image captures dynamics very difficult to depict in other ways. Integrative Meta-perspective, by helping make whole-box-of-crayons systemic understanding possible, offers a sophistication of thought that before now has not been an option. *Rethinking How We Think* examines both what Integrative Meta-perspective involves and why new, more whole-box-of-crayons ways of thinking have become essential.

Each chapter in the book comes at doing so from a slightly different direction. Chapter One introduces the kind of change process that produces Integrative Meta-perspective and examines how whole-box-of-crayons systemic understanding is the result. It then turns to some of the challenges that today most put the species at risk to illustrate needed new skills and capacities and how they will be critical going forward.

Chapter Two turns more specifically to the cognitive reordering that makes needed new ways of understanding possible. It examines the cognitive structures that gave us modern age beliefs, both why they have been so dramatically successful and also why they cannot continue to serve us in times ahead. It then looks at just what becomes different with Integrative Meta-perspective.

Chapter Three delves more deeply into Cultural Maturity's changes by examining the workings of human intelligence. It looks at how Integrative Meta-perspective makes it possible to more consciously draw on intelligence's multiple aspects and how whole-box-of-crayons systemic thinking is a result. It also examines how each of the new capacities that comes with Cultural Maturity's changes can be understood to follow from this essential new step in intelligence's evolution.

Chapter Four turns to applications and implications. It touches briefly on how Integrative Meta-perspective alters how we go about making choices. It then addresses how Integrative Meta-perspective brings essential insights for addressing critical collective challenges— from rethinking leadership and love, to recognizing the importance of a new maturity in our relationship to death, to appreciating what will be required if the digital revolution is to benefit us and not instead be our undoing.

Chapter Five takes on the topic of how Integrative Meta-perspective can best be supported and facilitated. Practicing needed new skills and capacities can take us a long way, but it turns out that there are also specific approaches that can be used to more directly generate the needed new cognitive structures. We will give some extended attention to one approach I have found particularly powerful, what CST calls simply Parts Work.

Chapter Six turns to how Integrative Meta-perspective ties to more overarching ideas such as those of Creative Systems Theory. We will look at how CST provides explanation for why Integrative Meta-perspective's cognitive reordering is now needed and also for how, in our time, it becomes possible. We will also see how CST, by offering a way to step beyond modern age machine-model assumptions, makes a major contribution to the larger history of ideas. As a bonus, we will look at how the way CST reframes truth helps us address not just current cultural concerns, but quite ultimate kinds of questions, questions that have always before left us baffled.

The Afterword's concluding observations return us to the easily paradoxical-seeming outcome that I pointed toward earlier, how while

Integrative Meta-perspective challenges us to make a major leap in understanding life's complexities, the picture that results can seem in important ways simpler, even rather like common sense. What we encounter reflects a maturity of common sense that before now we could have neither understood nor tolerated, but it follows directly from the more encompassing picture of understanding's evolution that becomes visible with Integrative Meta-perspective.

It is my hope that by the end of this book the concept of Integrative Meta-perspective will seem straightforward and obviously important. It is my hope, too, that you will have gained a solid beginning facility with making culturally mature understanding manifest both in your personal life and in whatever your larger cultural contribution may be.

CHAPTER ONE

Cultural Maturity and the Systemic Imperative

My efforts as a futurist are different from those of most people who concern themselves with the tasks ahead in a couple of key ways. The first has to do with the kinds of questions that most capture my attention. The greater portion of futurists focus on the technological—on innovations such as machine learning and genetic manipulation or the possibility of populating other planets. My primary interest lies with the human dimension. I'm concerned with the values we hold and how we think. And I'm interested in the narratives on which we base our actions—the stories we tell about who we are and what matters.

That my primary interest lies with the human dimension is only in part because of my background as a psychiatrist. It is also because the questions on which the future most depends are ultimately of this sort. Like it or not, few of the most important challenges ahead for the species have technological fixes. In addition, it is because the human dimension, perhaps surprisingly, is what we can say most about. While our track record when it comes to predicting invention is embarrassingly poor. we can say a great deal about the values and ways of understanding that advancing in an ultimately healthy and vital manner will require.

The second way that my contribution as a futurist is different is the topic of this book: the particular perspective I bring to addressing human questions. As I've introduced, by this I mean perspective in more than just the sense of approach. I mean it in terms of worldview, and even more fundamentally, in terms of the kind of cognitive orientation and organization that I bring to reflecting on the tasks ahead. My vantage is systemic, and systemic in the particularly encompassing and dynamic sense that becomes possible with Integrative Meta-perspective.

Introducing this vantage presents particular challenges due to the nature of the vantage itself. Certainly, the simple fact that understanding requires that the reader step into new conceptual territory adds to the difficulty. But, in addition, not only is this territory that the reader may not know exists, he or she may see no reason to expect it to exist. And there is more. Later we will see how the difficulty is further compounded by the fact that familiar approaches to explanation and depiction commonly fail us when we attempt to engage needed new ways of understanding.

Here I will touch on a couple of topics that help ease the transition before we turn to the specifics of Integrative Meta-perspective. First, I will address the general kind of change process that produces Integrative Meta-perspective and tie where it takes us more directly to whole-box-of-crayons systemic understanding. I will then turn to a small handful of challenges critical to humanity's future that highlight the need for new human skills and capacities and make the new kind of understanding that results with Integrative Meta-perspective obvious in its importance.

Truth, Developmental Change, and Whole-Box-of-Crayons Perspective

To get at how Integrative Meta-perspective relates to culturally mature understanding, we need to start by stepping back and reflecting a bit on understanding itself, on just what makes something true. We tend to think we know. We assume that truth is about knowing the facts. Or at the very least, we assume that the important thing is how intelligent we are in applying the facts.

But things aren't that simple. In fact, truth makes sense only if understood in relation to its context. And this is not just the case for ourselves. Ultimately what any creature assumes to be true depends on the lenses through which it makes sense of its world. A bear, a bee, or a bat certainly perceives a very different world than we do as humans. And for them and their needs, what they perceive is the more useful, and thus ultimately most accurate kind of truth.

This kind of conclusion applies to us humans in some particularly consequential ways. One way is how deeply what we see can depend on when we do the seeing. Here I mean "when" not just in the everyday sense of clock time, but more specifically in the sense of where we are developmentally. Such temporal relativity is familiar to us from our personal growing up—with how different the worldview of a child can be from that of an adult. As it turns out, not just what a child thinks, but how he or she thinks—the cognitive mechanisms the child draws on—differs fundamentally.

Creative Systems Theory takes this kind of observation further in a way that will have major importance in these reflections. It describes how we see related "developmental" sorts of differences with different periods in history. The world as seen through the eyes of a tribal hunter, a medieval mystic, or a modern scientist are not at all the same. And it is not just technologies—or even just beliefs—that have changed, though certainly they have. The cognitive mechanisms through which we perceive and understand have evolved with each new chapter in culture's story.

Because we are like fish in water, this kind of relativity can be very difficult to recognize from within the reality of a particular stage. And the difficulty is compounded by a couple of additional factors. With each new stage in understanding to this point, we've elevated and mythologized its conclusions—made its reality special. We've also assumed that those conclusions reflected truth's last word.

Both of these additional tendencies accompanied our most recent stage in culture's evolving story, that which has given us our Modern Age. Certainly we've considered modern age accomplishments to be special—with some legitimacy. The modern age worldview has served us powerfully, giving us institutions such as democratic government and higher education along with the Industrial Age and today's Information Age. We've also tended to think of modern age institutions and ways of thinking as ideals and end points.

Each of these tendencies can now present obstacles as we attempt to address challenges ahead for us as a species. Mythologizing gets in the way of seeing clearly what is in fact before us. And of particular significance when it comes to looking toward the future, our tendency to think of modern age institutions and ways of thinking as ideals and endpoints easily leaves us in denial when we encounter fissures appearing in modern age assumptions.

In fact, there is no reason to think of modern age beliefs and modern age institutions as some end of the road, and every reason to hope that they are not. It turns out that important questions ahead for the species are simply not addressable—or even adequately graspable—limited to modern age conclusions and ways of thinking. Shortly, we will look at how leaving such beliefs behind us and thinking in more sophisticated and complete ways has today become essential, and not just if we are to make better choices. If we can't think in new ways, we are most likely doomed.

CST argues that a further chapter in our human story is not just possible, it is predicted, at least if we can bring to bear the needed courage and commitment. To get at how this might be so and also to better make sense of what this essential further chapter in how we understand asks of us, it helps to look more closely at the sort of change process Integrative Meta-perspective involves. I've spoken of it as requiring a leap. This leap is of a particular sort, and particular in a couple of different ways.

The first way it is particular is shared by major transition points in any human developmental process. Even though this kind of change is familiar to us, it requires that we revisit how we commonly think about change. More conventionally, we assume change is either additive (with one step following logically from the one before) or transformational (all-or-nothing). Change that takes us between developmental stages is always in important ways both. We can think of it like crossing a threshold separating two worlds of experience. Such change continues a familiar process (growth), and at the same time it takes us into a wholly new world of experience.

The transition from modern age thought to culturally mature understanding is also particular in a way that we have not before witnessed, at least at a cultural level. Later we will examine how we find related mechanisms with the changes that give us second-half-of-life maturity in our personal development.[1] But it is unique to this time in culture's developmental story. And because it is happening at this most encompassing of scales, it reorders experience in a manner that is especially consequential.

The most immediate consequence is the change dynamic that gives the concept of Cultural Maturity its name. With Integrative Meta-

---

1 Chapter Three examines how we see related change dynamics with the midpoint of any human developmental process.

perspective, we leave behind relating to culture as a symbolic parent. By itself, this most immediate result has major implications. In times past, culture, like a good father or mother, has given us clear rules to live by. In doing so, it has provided us with a sense of identity and connectedness with others. It has also protected us from the immensity of life's uncertainties and complexities. With Integrative Meta-perspective, we step beyond such ready sureties.

But it is how Cultural Maturity's changes alter the way we think that will here most occupy our attention. Integrative Meta-perspective allows us to at once step back from, and more deeply engage, all the various aspects that make up our complex human natures. It offers that we might engage experience from the systemic whole of who we are in a way that before now would have made no sense to us. In the process, it gives us both more mature kinds of values and new, more dynamic and encompassing ways of understanding.

I've observed how making sense of Cultural Maturity's cognitive changes presents challenges not just because where they take us is new, but because of difficulties intrinsic to the task of depiction. It turns out that neither simple diagrams nor language, when applied in conventional ways, can quite get us there. Later, we will see how this difficulty—what CST calls the Dilemma of Representation—follows directly from just how needed new ways of thinking are new.

I'm always delighted when I find an image or a way of using language that can help.[2] I've found that simple box-of-crayons image particularly useful. It depicts being not just more inclusive in what we consider, but inclusive in a way that incorporates ingredients of wholly different sorts, getting our minds around apples-and-oranges distinctions. It also points toward how understanding changes fundamentally when we are able to step back and view a larger picture. The result with whole-box-of-crayons systemic understanding is not some mushing together or averaging of differences, but rather the ability to better appreciate and consciously draw on the whole of experience's multihued complexity.

---

2 CST calls images that help us get beyond the Dilemma of Representation "three-plus representation." Such images use three dimensions of depiction to represent what ultimately would require more than just this.

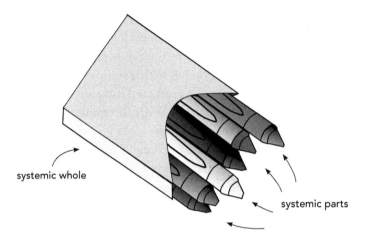

systemic whole

systemic parts

Fig. 1-1. "Whole-Box-of-Crayons" Systemic Understanding

To glimpse how fundamentally whole-box-of-crayons systemic per-spective differs from what we have known, we can turn to most any scale of understanding. Differences stand out most immediately when we apply it to specific cultural challenges, particularly ones where con-flicting ideologies come into play. CST defines ideology as any belief that takes one part of a larger systemic complexity—a single crayon— and makes it the whole of truth. Understood in this way, conflicting ideologies become not just opposing beliefs, but juxtaposed cognitive patterns within a particular cultural time's defining cognitive structure. We can think of the contrasting "red" and "blue" advocacies of politi-cal debate in this way as opposed systemic "crayons."

The significance of whole-box-of-crayons systemic perspective also becomes quickly apparent when we apply it to more encompass-ing concerns like the growing importance of global perspective or to thinking in ways that are more socially inclusive. The need for more interdisciplinary inquiry in academia provides especially provocative illustration. Later, I will describe ways in which the needed new kind of systemic thinking presents inherent challenges to academia and how one result is that academia today provides much less leadership when it comes to critical questions ahead for the species than we might hope.[3]

---

3 See Chapter Three.

And, as important, whole-box-of-crayons systemic perspective helps us better address our own complexity—ourselves as systems. In Chapter Three, I will give particular attention to a kind of multiplicity that CST identifies as being especially fundamental—the multiple intelligences/sensibilities that make up our cognitive functioning. Here the different "crayons" become human intelligence's multiple ways of knowing. In Chapter Five, I will use a related metaphor to speak more generally of inner experience's multiplicity. We will look at how one of the most powerful approaches for engaging Integrative Meta-perspective treats our inner lives like a play with many players.

With Integrative Meta-perspective, previous observations about understanding and truth continue to hold. The more whole-box-of-crayons picture that results doesn't provide final answers or truth in some ultimate sense. But what Integrative Meta-perspective does provide could not be more important. It offers a vantage that fundamentally alters our experience of ourselves and our worlds. With regard to the future, it gives us the more mature, encompassing, and dynamic ways of understanding on which good choices going forward will necessarily depend.

Challenges That Could Be Our Undoing

To effectively engage the concept of Integrative Meta-perspective, we need first to have a solid sense of why changes in how we think have become so important. A quick look at some of the most significant challenges confronting the species and the new skills and capacities needed to address them helps make the need for whole-box-of-crayons systemic perspective more understandable—even inescapable.

The challenges I have focused on in my various writings have ranged widely from front-page-news issues like terrorism, immigration, and gender relations to how we need to rethink whole domains of understanding, from education and government, to business, science, and religion. Here I will touch just briefly on a small handful of concerns that are alike in the potential they have to be our undoing as a species.

These examples are stark in their warnings. With each, failing to bring the needed maturity of perspective to bear will at least bring significant pain. The result could also be catastrophe. Together, they highlight the simple fact that unless a significant portion of the population can begin to manifest the new values and ways of understanding that Integrative Meta-perspective makes possible, life in times ahead will at best be decidedly unpleasant.

I will tie each concern to one of three key themes that run through the needed new skills and capacities: the importance of getting beyond us-versus-them assumptions, the need for a new maturity in our relationship to limits, and the essential task of learning to think about what matters in more complete ways. These themes, each in a different way, support the conclusion that the most important questions of our time are human questions. Each also brings emphasis to both the importance of new ways of understanding and how such understanding must be more encompassing, more systemic. And each at least begins to point toward how the needed systemic understanding is necessarily of the new, specifically whole-box-of-crayons sort that Integrative Meta-perspective makes possible.

How Us-Versus-Them Beliefs Could Be the End of Us

Our human tendency to see the world in us-versus-them terms plays a central role in a great many of today's most pressing human concerns. Certainly we recognize it in conflict between nations. But we see it too in political gridlock, and in racism, sexism, class divisions, and ethnic hatreds. In Chapter Three, I will describe how CST helps us understand not just why we have before thought in the language of polarity, but also why we have done so in specific ways at different times and places. Here our interest lies with the possibility of getting beyond this kind of thinking that has always before been a defining aspect of the human experience.

It is important not to view us-versus-them thinking as simply a reflection of human failing. In times past, it has served us. It has protected us from life's multihued complexities by reducing options to a more manageable black and white. And the absoluteness of its conclusions has similarly protected us from needing to confront uncertainties that before now would have been more than we could tolerate. But just as important today is the recognition that such protection no longer provides benefit. As we look to the future, if we hold to this historically common way of keeping experience manageable, the only result can be calamity.

The dangers are easiest to appreciate with relationships between nations. Throughout history, collective identity has depended on dividing the world into "chosen people" and "evil others." Doing so has served to solidify social bonds and protect us from truths that we have not yet been ready to accept. But we can't escape that such reactive mechanisms now threaten to have an opposite result. In our increasingly globalized world with readily available weapons of mass destruction, us-versus-them thinking on the global stage becomes inconsistent with survival. War at any scale has stopped being an option.

Like it or not, neither technological solutions nor simple changes in policy can save us from such consequences. We tend to miss how this is so in different ways depending on our political persuasion. We may assume that we can be safe if only we have the largest stockpile of arms. Or we can conclude with equal certainty that disarmament will provide the necessary answer. But while good defenses and reducing armaments each have a place, in the end, neither can protect us. Our only hope lies ultimately with getting beyond the chosen-people/evil-other mechanisms that traditionally have led to conflict.

Given human behavior to this point, this result might seem beyond anything we might hope to achieve. And the fact that many of the world's people today occupy cultural realities far from where needed more mature sensibilities could even be considered magnifies the task's difficulty. But leaving behind chosen-people/evil-other mechanisms can't be beyond us if any kind of optimism as we look to the future is to be warranted.

In fact, there are good reasons to think needed changes are possible. We can derive at least limited encouragement from accomplishments already realized. I think, most immediately, of the fall of the Berlin Wall. In the end, the Berlin Wall fell not because one side had prevailed, but because people had grown tired of what the wall represented. And that is not the only example. In *Cultural Maturity: A Guidebook for the Future*, I argue that the modern West would likely have responded much more dangerously and reactively to the threat of terrorism if we were not seeing at least the beginnings of more mature sensibilities.

More specifically there is how Cultural Maturity's cognitive reordering directly supports the needed changes. Integrative Meta-perspective helps us get beyond the polarizations and simplifications that in times past have led to war. It invites us to think in the more mature and complete ways needed if conflicts between nations are not to result in catastrophe.

Our box-of-crayons metaphor helps clarify just how this is so. With mythologized thinking, we elevate certain "crayons" and demonize others. In relationships between nations, we've identified with the elevated crayons and projected the demonized crayons, making them attributes of peoples we perceived to be different from ourselves. With Integrative Meta-perspective, we become newly able to own the whole box. We better appreciate the various crayons as aspects of ourselves. We also recognize that other systems similarly manifest such multifaceted complexity.

In keeping with the apparent paradox that I noted in the Preface, while Integrative Meta-perspective requires that we think more complexly than we have in times past, it also in important ways makes things simpler. The picture that results is more complex in that it requires us to give up the idealizations and projections that before have protected us from the fact of real differences and how complicated relationships can be.[4] And at the same time, in important ways it is more straightforward, more common sense. Instead of seeing the world through the distorting lens of mythologized truths, we come a critical step closer to seeing things for just how they are.

Us-versus-them ideological beliefs that manifest at smaller scales, such as in the political arena, might seem to present less immediate concern, but the dangers may ultimately be just as great. In times past, such thinking again has served us. At the least, in a related way it has protected us from complexity and uncertainty.[5] But more local us-versus-them thinking, too, is ceasing to provide benefit.

I find the degree of partisan pettiness and polarization we so often witness today seriously worrisome. Polarization has reached such an extreme that often very little of substance can get accomplished. It is reasonable to fear that if we can't get beyond it, not only will we fail to advance further beyond modern age assumptions, we might regress

---

4   While we tend to assume polarized conflict is about difference—indeed, extreme difference—in fact, because projection involves attributing aspects of ourselves to another system, polarization functions to protect us from the experience of real difference.

5   And CST suggests deeper kinds of benefit. In *Cultural Maturity: A Guidebook for the Future*, I describe how the alternating of liberal and conservative tendencies has in times past worked to drive creative change.

and lose the essential progress we have made in recent centuries. In the worst-case scenario, functional government may become impossible and we could see the end of the democratic experiment.

Here again the possibility of getting beyond us-versus-them reactiveness might initially seem only to be wishful thinking. But just as the polarizations that lead to war are based on projection rather than on accurate perceptions of difference, so too are the polarizations that produce partisan gridlock. Ultimately, they are more about the clashing of opposite-hued crayons than reasoned reflection, or even the kind of impassioned debate we may find with real differences of opinion.

The notion that political polarization has more to do with our cognitive mechanisms than the real complexities of policy can for many people seem radical. At the least it comes as a surprise. We find some of the best evidence in the way issues that later become highly polarized are often not thought of in partisan terms at all when they first come to the public's attention.[6] Indeed, it is frequently not clear what the "sides" would be, much less who would take them, if the issue did become politicized. Only later do battle lines get drawn.

The common closeness of elections provides another kind of evidence. If voting were based on the perceived intelligence of the candidate's ideas, we would see general agreement as to which candidate is the most qualified much more often than we do. Instead, elections are most often won by a few percentage points, or less. This is what we would predict if we are dealing not just with differences of opinion, but polar opposite cognitive patterns.

I have a blog and also a podcast site where I take on the role of "cultural psychiatrist" and endeavor to bring culturally mature perspective

---

6 This was the case, for example, with both climate change and health care reform. There were no obvious sides to the climate change debate when the evidence first came to light. And the approach on which Obamacare was initially modeled was Republican Mitt Romney's plan in Massachusetts. We often encounter related surprises with us-versus-them antagonisms on the world stage. It turns out that wars are less often the result of major differences than we tend to assume. Think of how World War I began with the assassination of Austro-Hungarian heir Archduke Franz Ferdinand. While it was a significant event, few people had any idea it could have such world-altering consequences.

to contemporary issues.[7] When a social concern becomes highly polarized—as we've see in recent years, for example, with health care reform,
abortion, climate change, immigration, or issues of gender and appropriate sexual behavior—I attempt to step back and engage the concern
from a more encompassing vantage.

A series of recognitions that follow from the whole-box-of-crayons
nature of needed answers inevitably comes into play. First, while each
polar position holds at least a small a piece of the truth, neither can
provide ultimately useful solutions (each reflects a crayon). Second,
each position in the end stops short of recognizing the hard question
that needs to be addressed (the question being systemic in nature, it
can only be grasped from a larger vantage). And third, compromise
between polarized positions ultimately gets us no closer to where we
need to go (splitting the difference between crayons is very different
from holding the whole box).

With any issue, I start by attempting to identify the hard question
that neither position effectively recognizes. This in itself does not sup-
ply needed solutions, but it does mean that our inquiry will at least be
in the right territory. As solutions do begin to take shape, we generally
find that each of the opposing positions has at least something useful to
contribute. But we also find that any kind of useful contribution requires
the holder of the original position to surrender basic assumptions.[8]

I've noted how partisan pettiness today threatens to take us back-
wards and put the modern age democratic experiment at risk. Certainly,
it will get in the way of effectively moving forward as a species. Functional government in the long term will depend on the kind of whole-
box-of-crayons systemic understanding Cultural Maturity's cognitive
changes make possible. Effective future governance will require leaders

---

7   See www.culturalmaturityblog.net and www.lookingtothefuture.net.

8   Over the course of this book, I will apply this kind of systemic teasing apart
    to a variety of contemporary front-page-news concerns, including many of
    those just noted. I will also touch on a handful of more philosophical topics
    that traditionally get framed in polar terms: the often conflicting world-
    views of science and religion, the apparent contradiction between free will
    and determinism, and how we best understand the relationship between
    humankind and the natural world.

able to hold issues more systemically and voters who are interested in supporting leaders capable of doing so. It may also require new, more systemically conceived governmental structures.[9] What we can know is that without more whole-box-of-crayons ways of understanding, we will simply not be able to make the kinds of more mature and systemic decisions on which effective governance going forward will depend.

A simple way to further appreciate how the challenges we face have to do with understanding itself—with the workings of our cognitive mechanisms and not just beliefs or policies—is to turn our attention to moral quandaries. Moral questions also help us more fully get our minds around what the needed, more specifically whole-box-of-crayons kind of understanding involves. We can miss that political concerns, and social issues of every sort, in the end engage us in moral decision-making.

Moral quandaries have a fascinating shared characteristic, one that up until now most people have failed to recognize. They are never really about right versus wrong or good versus evil. If they were, they would not be quandaries. Rather moral quandaries confront us with competing goods.

The abortion question provides an obvious example. It juxtaposes the sanctity of choice and the sanctity of life. Each of these values reflect a fundamental good. We have viewed them in polarized terms only because the complexity and uncertainty that inherently comes with seeing them more accurately and systemically would in times past have been more than we could tolerate.

And there is more. A second essential characteristic of moral quandaries helps point toward the particular kind of systemic perspective today's challenges require of us. The competing goods inherent in difficult moral questions almost always juxtapose choices of an apples-and-oranges sort. Thus they aren't reconcilable simply by splitting the difference. We can't solve the abortion debate by having the two sides meet halfway.

Grasp these two essential truths and we've come a long way toward the needed more mature kind of systemic understanding. We can think of all the most important questions of our time as moral questions, including major overarching social questions such as those that confront us with

---

9 See *Cultural Maturity: A Guidebook for the Future* or "Government and Governance" in the ICD blog library.

relations between nations and political partisanship—in the end, they are questions of value. And because they most often involve multiple apples-and-oranges considerations, they are questions that require more than just thinking harder, even if we take conflicting positions into account. Important questions of every sort today require that we engage them in the new, more encompassing, whole-box-of-crayons, systemic ways that Integrative Meta-perspective makes possible.

We can sum up this first theme with a simple lesson. In times past, when we encountered polarized positions and partisan advocacy, our task was obvious and unquestioned. We assumed that there were only two options and that our task was to fight for the side that was right. With Integrative Meta-perspective, the recognition of polarity has very different implications. It alerts us to the fact that we need to expand our vantage, see a big enough picture. When we do, we recognize that neither side is yet asking the hard question that ultimately needs to be answered. We also recognize that while each side may hold a piece of the truth, neither side by itself, nor some simple compromise between sides, can get us where we need to go.

The Fact of Real Limits and the Possibility of Ecological Catastrophe

For many people, it is the threat of ecological catastrophe that most conjures up images of our undoing. Take your pick—climate change, the growing rate of species extinctions, the loss of needed resources such as adequate food supplies or clean air and water.

Any of these circumstances by themselves could result in immense harm. And any one could readily combine with other challenges to create even more dangerous realities. For example, one of the greatest risks with climate change is that the disruptions that come with warming temperatures will increase conflict on the planet and with this the likelihood of the use of weapons of mass destruction.

To effectively address the possibility of ecological catastrophe, we must first recognize that once again we are dealing not just with a technological challenge, but with what is ultimately a human challenge. Further development of renewable energy sources and the achievement of greater energy efficiency will have clear roles in responding to these dangers. But in the end, whether we are successful at avoiding environmental devastation will be a function of our human choices.

We also need again to recognize that choosing and acting effectively will depend on capacities new to us as a species. Most immediately, doing so will require a capacity for foresight and concern for the long term that we have not before witnessed.[10] Put simply, it will demand a new, more grown-up kind of responsibility. This same greater responsibility is ultimately needed if we are to effectively get beyond the us-versus-them beliefs of times past, but the fact that the consequences with environmental catastrophe so directly concern not just our human well-being but the well-being of life as a whole brings particular emphasis to its newness and importance.

Making needed choices will also depend on a further, more specific new capacity. We must learn to better appreciate the fact of real limits. We can effectively address environmental dangers only if we can accept that there are real limits to resources. We also have to accept that there are certain things that we simply can't continue to do. And we have to face that there are also real limits to what we as humans can understand and control.[11]

Besides highlighting the need to acknowledge limits in especially stark ways, the possibility of environmental catastrophe also brings particularly direct attention to the importance of thinking more systemically. Words like "ecological" and "environmental" refer specifically to the importance of considering contexts and interconnections. Environmental limits also help further fill out our understanding of the particular sort of systemic thinking the future depends on. They directly confront us with the importance of having systems ideas that can effectively address living systems.

Mechanical systems may break if they are pushed too far, but they can usually be fixed, and designs can always be refined and improved. With living systems, real limits are inherent to how things work. Bears can't fly, and the result if a bear believes otherwise is not going to be pretty. Make a creature too hot or too cold and it will not long survive. With living systems, inviolable limits come with the territory. Ignore them and life ceases to exist.

---

10 Note that we have all before taken classes on the past, but very few people have had classes on the future.

11 Again this is a new capacity I have written about extensively. *Cultural Maturity: A Guidebook for the Future* provides the most detailed analysis.

Our relationship to limits changes fundamentally with Integrative Meta-perspective. How it does follows directly from the way Integrative Meta-perspective draws on the entirety of who we are as systems. From the more whole-box-of-crayons, life-acknowledging and human-life-acknowledging vantage that results, that fact of limits becomes obvious, and obviously important to always take into account.

Given that the fact of real limits might seem obvious, it is reasonable to ask why the ability to acknowledge them has thus far been so difficult for us. Again we come back to how we think—or rather, how we have thought in times past. Modern age narratives have most often been of one of two sorts—either heroic or romantic. Heroic and romantic narratives each celebrate limitlessness. Heroic narratives proclaim that if only we sufficiently persevere, any obstacle can be transcended. Romantic narratives promise that if we find the right kind of connectedness—with another person, with nature, with some particular poetic or spiritual belief—anything can be possible.

Like beliefs that divide humanity into chosen people and evil others, myths of limitlessness, in their time, have served us. They've supported the modern age emphasis on individual achievement and have helped get us beyond the constraining prohibitions of the Middle Ages. They've also protected us from recognitions—for example, about what is possible and what is not—that before now we would have found too much to handle. But these same once-inspiring stories, also today similarly invite calamity. If we can't come to grips with the fact of real limits, we will fail to address not just environmental challenges, but most any of the really important questions of our time.

Later in the book, we will look at how a new maturity in a relationship to limits will be central to success with all manner of future challenges, from leading and loving in ways that can work, to designing effective health care systems, to effectively managing emerging technologies. Integrative Meta-perspective makes clear that recognizing where real limits may exist is one of the necessary first steps if we wish to engage a question in a culturally mature way. Historically, acknowledging limits would be interpreted as failure or weakness. From Integrative Meta-perspective's more systemic vantage, the recognition of inviolable limits becomes key to success and the making of wise—and thus ultimately powerful—choices.

We can sum up this second theme again with a simple lesson. Prior to now, when we encountered limits, we have assumed that our task was to heroically (or romantically) break through them. With Integrative Meta-perspective, we first pause and take time to discern just what kind of limit we face. If it is a limit that warrants a more traditional response, we proceed as before—and with added conviction. But we are also open to the possibility that the limit is inviolable. In a culturally mature reality, making this kind of distinction becomes a central task of leadership in all parts of our personal and collective lives.

Asking What Matters More Systemically and
Confronting Today's Crisis of Narrative

The last of our examples in important ways encompasses all the others. If we are to effectively advance, we need to rethink what advancement should entail. A simple way to put it is that we need new, more systemic, more whole-box-of-crayons measures for wealth and progress. Our modern age definitions are so familiar that we tend not to question them. Wealth is the accumulation of material assets. And progress is new inventions and economic growth. Today, if we don't question them—and question them fundamentally—the consequences will be dire.

As with us-versus-them beliefs and the heroic and romantic myths of times past, thinking about advancement as we have in modern times has benefitted us. Our familiar definition of wealth has been closely tied to our modern concept of the individual. And defining progress as we have has been central to the wondrous achievements of the Industrial Age and the great power of modern economies. But as with these other aspects of the modern age worldview, while our familiar definitions of wealth and progress might seem logical, they are products primarily of how we have thought in times past. And in a similar way, they cannot continue to provide benefit going forward.

When I want to help a person get at what more is needed, I will often first engage them at a personal level. I will ask them to talk to me about what creates meaning—"wealth" in the largest sense—in their individual lives. Most people mention money, but most recognize too that beyond a certain point money is less tied to meaning than one might think. Invention, too, most always has a place—people like their gadgets. But most people recognize that other things are ultimately as important, or often much more important: one's family, one's friends, one's community, one's felt relationship with nature, one's creative and intellectual pursuits.

People doing this exercise are often surprised to find that a significant mismatch exists between what they have described as most important for a meaningful life and many of their day-to-day choices. I may joke with the person as they confront this recognition, pointing out—only partly tongue in cheek—that this kind of discrepancy would seem to be almost the definition of insanity. When working in therapy, this kind of recognition can result in people making major life changes.

Later we may engage this same kind of inquiry in relation to how more collectively we think of wealth and progress. In doing so, the degree to which our current world circumstances reflect a related kind of mismatch becomes hard to escape. Too often today we hold to an outmoded definition of advancement that excludes much that is in fact most important to us. Just as we appropriately think of an individual who makes choices that are not in keeping with what the person finds most important as deranged, the implications are huge. Later in the book, we will look closely at how taking the modern age narrative beyond its timeliness threatens to distance us from much that most matters to us in quite fundamental ways.[12]

I've often given particular attention in my writing to a specific result that follows from this circumstance, what CST calls our time's Crisis of Purpose. I introduced my recent book *Hope and the Future: Confronting Today's Crisis of Purpose* by describing therapy work with a young man who had attempted to hang himself. It became strikingly clear in our conversations that the hopelessness he felt was only in limited ways personal. It was more about the state of the world. He described having a hard time thinking of a future he would want to be a part of. The aspects of therapy that most helped him involved asking together what a meaningful human future might look like, exploring how we would need to rethink the human story to get there, and him asking how he in his life might contribute to that new story.

In our time, we find marked increases in rates of depression and suicide. We also witness increasing rates of addiction, and not just

---

12 See the discussion of the Dilemma of Trajectory in Chapter Three.

substance addiction as with the opioid crisis, but addiction to consumption as we see with the obesity epidemic, and I suspect of greatest long-term concern, addiction to distraction and artificial stimulation as we see with how addiction to electronic devices has today come to be in effect a social norm.[13]

How do we best think about needed new measures for wealth and progress? For our task here, the central recognition is that they must be of our more whole-box-of-crayons systemic sort. Whole-box-of-crayons measures will be required if we are to successfully assess the benefits and risks of new technologies. (We need such measures if we are to effectively determine what we are to call benefit.) Such measures will similarly be critical to making good environmental decisions. (It is only through them that we can appreciate how impoverished further environmental destruction would leave us.) And, certainly, more mature and systemic measures for wealth and progress will be necessary if we are to effectively address the ever-widening gap between the world's haves and have-nots. (Ask about benefit more consciously and we begin to better recognize how such disparities are not just ethically troubling, but risk destabilizing societies and putting everyone's well-being in peril.)

We can think of the task of redefining wealth and progress as a particularly encompassing example of a more basic kind of challenge that confronts us with culturally mature questions of every sort. Earlier I described the third essential change theme as learning to think about what matters in more complete ways. Confronting any kind of important concern necessarily starts with asking what most matters to us in doing so, addressing what CST calls the pertinent Question of Referent. Once over Cultural Maturity's threshold, referents that work are necessarily of a more integrative, whole-box-of-crayons, systemic sort. Redefining wealth and progress engages the task of addressing today's Question of Referent for humanity as a whole.

The concept of Cultural Maturity offers an answer to humanity's now defining Question of Referent. At its heart is a more complete

---

13 In Chapter Four, I will address device addiction specifically, and in particular how both understanding it and confronting it successfully relate to holding intelligence in the more systemic and complete way that Integrative Meta-perspective makes possible.

appreciation of all that matters to us in being human. Integrative Meta-perspective offers that we might learn to live consciously from such more complete understanding and thus have the greatest chance of effectively advancing as a species.

We can sum up this third theme, like the others, with a simple lesson. Historically, when making decisions, we would look to culturally prescribed truths. With modern times, we've also looked specifically to prescribed truths of a materialist/individualist/objectivist sort. With Cultural Maturity, truths become ours to determine. At the most encompassing of scales, this truth task challenges us to define wealth and progress in more complete and ultimately life-affirming ways. Our future well-being as a species depends on it.

Integrative Meta-Perspective and the Long Term

Each of the three themes I've touched on are today pertinent to challenges of every sort and in every part of our lives. Here I've given particular attention to how they are essential to avoiding major harm. With each of the potentially calamitous circumstances I have noted, the necessary antidote to destruction lies with new kinds of capacities that become possible with Cultural Maturity's cognitive reordering.

Ultimately, it is not just that today's realities put us at risk. One or more of the calamitous circumstances I have described become inevitable if we fail to manifest the needed maturity of perspective. I could imagine sitting in a cave centuries from now with a group of survivors, contemplating what might have been. Certainly our conversation would include regret that we had not applied the needed wisdom early on when it could have made all the difference.

This book's reflections will engage us not just in thinking that is more long-term than we are used to, but in thinking that is long-term in a quite ultimate sense. Its conclusions are pertinent to decisions we must make in decades immediately ahead, certainly, but also to our choices well into the future. Indeed, CST proposes that today's initial engagements with more mature kinds of understanding are providing the groundwork for a filling out of who we are that should continue to be pertinent through the whole of our human existence.[14] Whether or

---

14 I will establish this conclusion more conceptually in Chapter Three.

not this conclusion is accurate, Integrative Meta-perspective should certainly be essential to any kind of world we would want to live in as far into the future as we can currently imagine.

We turn now more specifically to Integrative Meta-perspective, how it differs from what we have known, its underlying mechanisms, and how it produces the kind of changes I've described. The more complete engagement with experience Integrative Meta-perspective makes possible would before now have been too much for us to tolerate. Increasingly, everything else depends on it.

CHAPTER TWO

Integrative Meta-Perspective

We now have a solid beginning sense of how the changes that give us Integrative Meta-perspective are inescapably necessary. Later, we will look more closely at how they are predicted from the way change processes in human systems work more generally. Here our interest lies with Integrative Meta-perspective itself—its mechanisms and how specifically it alters understanding.

These further reflections will often draw on a key way in which Integrative Meta-perspective assists us beyond what we have examined thus far. In making frameworks like CST possible, it not only provides the basis for needed new ways of thinking, it also offers that we might better understand why we have thought in the remarkably different ways we have at different times in culture's story. It invites us to rewrite the past along with the present and the future. Here it will help us put Cultural Maturity's cognitive reordering in historical perspective and appreciate what makes the kind of understanding that results fundamentally different from what we have known.

With this chapter, we will first look in more detail at the cognitive reordering that produces Integrative Meta-perspective. We will then more closely examine the whole-box-of-crayons sort of systemic understanding that Integrative Meta-perspective generates for some important compare-and-contrast reflections. Finally, we will turn to a couple of additional ways of framing where Integrative Meta-perspective's changes take us that help us clearly distinguish what culturally mature understanding is and is not.

Cultural Maturity's Cognitive Reordering

Integrative Meta-perspective is new—and fundamentally so—but each major new chapter in culture's evolving story has similarly been marked by leaps in how we understand. The leap that brought us modern age thought provides the most pertinent comparison. The new sensibilities introduced with the fresh artistic visions of Michelangelo and Leonardo da Vinci in the fifteenth century and later filled out with seventeenth-century conceptual formulations such as Newton's clockworks universe and Descartes's emphasis on rationality as truth's last word did more than just alter our conclusions. They reflected a whole new kind of understanding—indeed, a new type of conceptual organization.

We can summarize what then became different with the simple observation that these changes made possible a new, more from-a-balcony kind of perspective—what we commonly refer to when we use the word "objective." Everything we tend to identify with modern age advancement—the rise of individualism, more democratic governmental forms, the Industrial Revolution, scientific preeminence, modern higher education, and a more personal conception of the divine—can be understood to follow from this basic cognitive reorganization and the new kind of vantage it produced.

In a similar way, we can make sense of everything about culturally mature understanding—what it asks of us, why it does so, and why we might expect the specific changes it describes—in terms of changes in the mechanisms through which we make sense of ourselves and the world around us. The cognitive reorganization that happens at Cultural Maturity's threshold—that which produces Integrative Meta-perspective—is related, but also new in basic ways.

I find it helpful to think of these changes as a two-part process, though in the end the two parts represent aspects of a single change dynamic. The first process engages us in a more complete kind of stepping back. The second, more specifically integrative process gives us the new depth of engagement necessary for the more complete kind of understanding that mature—wise—decision-making requires.

With the first kind of process, what we step back from has multiple aspects. Most immediately, we step back from ourselves as cultural beings. As we do, we become newly able to recognize culture's previous mythologized, "parental" status, and to begin moving beyond it. But cultural assumptions are not all we step back from. We also step back from internal aspects of ourselves in ways that were not possible before. I've emphasized the importance of being newly conscious of parts of ourselves that before we've projected, such as those we attribute to people who are different from ourselves when we see our worlds in us-versus-them terms.

Of particular importance in this picture is how we become more able to step back from intelligence's multiple aspects. Modern age belief made one aspect of intelligence—the rational—the ideal and end point in understanding (or with the romantic thread in understanding, rationality's opposite in the subjective). But rationality by itself is not enough. And obviously it can't be, if we look at all that goes into human experience and all that ultimately matters to us. Integrative Meta-perspective affirms the importance of rationality. But it also clarifies how rationality represents only one aspect of intelligence. It also brings emphasis to how each of intelligence's multiple aspects plays a key role in making us who we are.

I will address intelligence's multiplicity in more detail in the next chapter. For now, it is enough to note that besides the rational—in which we take appropriate pride—intelligence also has more emotional, imaginal, and bodily aspects. Each works according to different mechanisms and makes different kinds of contributions. With Integrative Meta-perspective, we are able to recognize whole-box-of-crayons complexity in the world because we more consciously and more fully draw on this larger complexity in ourselves.

The particular way our relationship with intelligence's multiplicity changes with Cultural Maturity's stepping-back process helps distinguish it from what has taken place at previous major cultural change points. Stepping back from more familiar ways of knowing played a similarly central role, for example, in the kind of cognitive reorganization that gave us modern age understanding. Modern age perspective distanced us from the more mystical sensibilities that had permeated the beliefs of the Middle Ages. But this distancing was achieved by a polar separating of the rational from more non-rational aspects of experience. It also involved allying conscious awareness specifically with rationality. Modern age truth's from-a-balcony sense of final clarity was achieved by separating experience into polar-opposite "objective" and "subjective" worlds.

The first part of Cultural Maturity's cognitive reordering continues the kind of stepping-back process that gave us modern age thought—and in an important sense also completes it. Awareness comes to stand separate from the whole of our intelligence's systemic complexity—now including the rational. In doing so, it takes us beyond identification with particular intelligences, a characteristic of each previous cultural stage.[1] It also begins to take us beyond thinking in the language of polarity. With culturally mature perspective, we step back equally from sensibilities we've before thought of as subjective and from ways of thinking that we've before identified with objectivity.

But this more complete stepping back gets us only part of the way. We also need that second, more specifically integrative kind of change process if the result is going to be the kind of thinking necessary for the tasks ahead. While the first aspect of Cultural Maturity's cognitive reordering effectively moves us beyond the most obvious of beliefs that take one part of a larger systemic dynamic and make it the whole of truth, at some level we know it is not enough. That more complete stepping back can at first feel exhilarating, but it can also feel precarious—stepping back this fully can leave us feeling strangely distanced from ourselves. Later, we will look at how these dynamics produce postmodern anything-goes moral relativism, techno-utopian blindnesses, and a variety of other dynamics that leave us short of where we need to go and often get directly in the way of what is needed.[2]

---

1 Chapter Three looks more closely at the relationship between aspects of intelligence and cultural stage.

2 Again see Chapter Three.

Not only is the second process I have pointed toward necessary if our thinking is to again have coherence and provide useful direction, at least a bit of it is necessary if we are simply to appreciate the fact of projective dynamics or the importance of a more complex picture of intelligence. What it involves is not just different from what we have known before, it finds no parallel at all in previous cultural change points. Along with more fully stepping back from the multiple aspects of our human complexity, Cultural Maturity's cognitive changes also involve more directly engaging that complexity. We plumb experience with a fundamentally new kind of depth. In the process, we come to more consciously and fully embody all that makes us who we are. This second part of Cultural Maturity's cognitive reordering produces Cultural Maturity's specifically systemic outcome.

We can think of what we more deeply engage in terms of any aspect of our human complexity. Once more, we can think of it, for example, in terms of reconnecting with aspects of ourselves that we've previously disowned and projected onto the world around us. But framing the result in terms of intelligence's multiplicity again helps get at what is most basic.

Describing intelligence as I have—as including not just rationality, but also more affective, imaginal, and bodily aspects—in fact required that I get ahead of myself. More than just stepping back from intelligence's multiplicity is needed to appreciate these multiple aspects with any depth. We also need this second process's more specifically integrative dynamics. Culturally mature understanding's conscious application of multiple aspects of intelligence becomes possible only with an essential kind of reengagement with sensibility in its entirety.[3]

The diagram in Figure 2-1 depicts the dual process that gives us Integrative Meta-perspective.

---

3 In Chapter Three, I will describe how amnesias inherent to the workings of formative process make an explicit process of reengagement necessary.

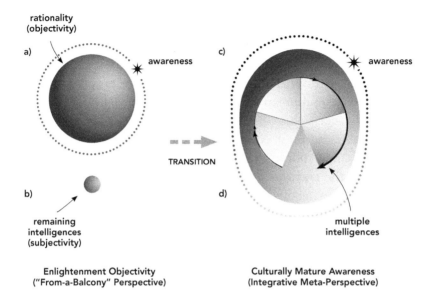

a) Rational intelligence (allied with awareness to produce from-a-balcony objectivity)

b) The subjective (all remaining intelligences as experienced in modern age reality)

c) < ------ * --------- >   Culturally mature awareness in its various more and less conscious permutations[4]

d) Multiple intelligences (made newly explicit with culturally mature perspective)

Fig. 2-1. Integrative Meta-Perspective[5]

---

4   It is important to appreciate how being maturely conscious is not the same as being conscious of everything—a topic we will return to when I address the role of conscious awareness in Chapter Six. We can begin to recognize how this is so in the way different intelligences tend to involve different degrees of conscious involvement.

5   The relationship of poles on the left side of the diagram reflects what we see with modern age dynamics. (See www.CSTHome.org for a more detailed look at this diagram.)

Our box-of-crayons image helps bring the two aspects of Cultural Maturity's cognitive reordering together. With Integrative Meta-perspective, we become newly able to step back from the rich multiplicity that underlies human understanding—intelligence's multiplicity, but also our multifaceted natures more broadly—all the hues that make up human sensibility. And we become able both to more deeply access this complexity of hues and to draw on its various aspects in the most creative ways. We both more consciously acknowledge and more directly draw on the whole of ourselves as systems—all the crayons in the box. With time, Cultural Maturity's cognitive reordering makes whole-box-of-crayons perspective seem like common sense.

I've observed that we see a related kind of cognitive reordering with the dynamics that mark second-half-of-life development in our individual lifetimes. Later in the chapter, I will draw on this observation to put flesh on these bare conceptual bones. For now, it is enough to note that second-half-of-life changes in our personal lives are what offer that we might be not just intelligent in our choices, but now and then also wise. Integrative Meta-perspective offers the possibility of being wise not just as individuals, but as a species. It is this that makes Integrative Meta-perspective the only option going forward—in the end, the only game in town.

Culturally Mature Systemic Thought

While our box of crayons metaphor does a remarkably good job of capturing where Integrative Meta-perspective takes us, it helps to think more conceptually if we wish to fully grasp how the result with Integrative Meta-perspective differs from other ways of understanding. Drawing in more detail on the language of systems helps us do so.

What exactly is systems thinking? Put most simply, it is thinking that attempts to consciously take into account everything involved—the whole ball of wax. Importantly, it concerns itself not just with parts but also with connectedness. "The whole is greater than the sum of its parts" is a familiar systems thinking rallying cry. Formal systems thinking first made its appearance in the early part of the last century. Its beginnings are most often associated with

Austrian biologist Karl Ludwig von Bertalanffy whose insights we
will explore a bit later in this section.[6]

The kind of systems thinking we have interest in with Integrative
Meta-perspective has important relationships to formal systems thinking's evolution over the last hundred years, but it also goes beyond what
we have seen to this point. To understand just how, it helps to begin
even further back. While formal systems thinking is new, we can also
think of systems sensibilities as having a long and venerated tradition.
In one sense, systems thinking is what engineers have always drawn
on from the crafting of the pyramids and Europe's great cathedrals to
modern times.

Language that I introduced in the previous chapter—how we
can think of modern age narrative as having heroic and romantic
threads—helps bring more detail to needed distinctions. (To have additional language, we could also describe these as the more "archetypally masculine"—or simply more right-hand—and more "archteypally
feminine"—or simply more left-hand— conceptual traditions.[7]) Both
heroic and romantic cognitive patterns can result in thinking that is
at least in ways "systemic." Contrasting where the heroic/archetypally
masculine and romantic/archetypally feminine threads in modern age
thought take us with what is being required in our time helps bring
focus to just what is new.

The more limited kind of systems thinking that comes from the
heroic thread in modern age thought simply affirms the mechanistic
assumptions we have historically drawn on when tackling technical

---

6 I draw on systems thinking as a way in not so much because of Creative Systems Theory's importance in these reflections, but because of the challenge
   systems thinking presents so effectively highlights what makes new ways
   of thinking new and helps make needed comparisons. In fact, the theory
   had its origins before I had any knowledge of systems thinking. CST was
   originally called the Theory of Creative Causality.

7 It is important to clearly distinguish this language of gender archetype from
   conclusions about gender. Both men and women embody both archetypally
   masculine and archetypally feminine qualities. My book *On the Evolution
   of Intimacy* looks in detail at this distinction. It also examines how our
   relationship to such archetypal qualities have evolved over the course of
   history.

problems. Such perspective can effectively address a complex array of parts and often complicated relationships. But the parts are ultimately of the same basic sort—no apples and oranges here. And the relationships are ultimately mechanical relationships, connectedness in the limited sense of actions and their predicted reactions.

We can similarly think of more romantic thought as systemic, but again in a specifically more limited sense than is our concern. Whether the focus is romantic love, the specifically poetic relationship with nature that came with nineteenth-century romanticism, or sensibilities of a more religious sort, the romantic thread in modern age thought brings attention to connectedness. Two essential differences distinguish such thought from what we have interest in. This is connectedness of a specifically magical sort—we know nothing about what actually makes the connection. And in the end, connectedness here is what it is all about. If difference is acknowledged as having any significance, its status is clearly secondary.

Von Bertalanffy recognized the importance of getting beyond both of these now-outmoded ways of thinking. But even more important was a key insight with regard to what success with the systemic task would need to accomplish. He saw that what had been missing was the ability to address living systems in ways that honored that they were alive, the ability to talk about living systems in living terms.[8] Von Bertalanffy failed at his dream of putting together a detailed formal systems formulation that succeeded at this task, but his initial observations made a powerful contribution.[9]

---

8 Ludwig von Bertalanffy, *General Systems Theory*, 1968, George Braziller.

9 Any at all detailed look at how systems thinking has evolved over the course of the last century is well beyond the scope of this short book, but one observation has particular pertinence. While further steps in systems thinking's development also made important contributions, none succeeded any better than the ideas of von Bertalanffy at providing detailed formulations that effectively addressed the workings of living systems. The cybernetics of Norbert Wiener and colleagues delineated the mechanisms of feedback loops and their role in self-regulation. Later, the sciences of complexity—chaos theory being the most familiar example—highlighted how uncertainty need not be inconsistent with order and brought further attention to how systems could self-organize. But each of these formulations remained basically

In the previous chapter, I made reference to the Dilemma of Representation and the way it contributes to how difficult it can be to talk about culturally mature perspective. A related "dilemma" described by CST—what the theory calls the Dilemma of Differentiation—both further highlights the challenge and helps clarify how the needed more dynamic and complete kind of conception becomes impossible to achieve if we are limited to the assumptions of either the heroic or the romantic conceptual traditions. In the process, it helps make more understandable why what von Bertalanffy hoped to achieve presents such a challenge and also what succeeding at the task necessarily requires.

The Dilemma of Differentiation describes the inherent difficulty of thinking with detail when it comes to living systems. It includes two contrasting recognitions. First, it observes that dividing a system up in any conventional sense in the end leaves us back in a machine world. This recognition immediately challenges any approach that draws on understanding of only a more heroic/archetypally masculine/right-hand sort. But the Dilemma of Differentiation also makes clear that just saying aspects of a system are interconnected by itself tells us very little. Differentiation is key to life. And the ability to distinguish this from that is what makes thinking useful. This second recognition just as fundamentally challenges any approach that draws only on understanding of a more romantic/archetypally feminine/left-hand sort.

Integrative Meta-perspective offers that we might think in ways that get beyond the Dilemma of Differentiation. We can again draw on our box-of-crayons metaphor to understand just how this is the case. With whole-box-of-crayons systemic thinking, some of the crayons identify more with difference, others more with interconnectedness, and they do so in a variety of apples-and-oranges ways. The recognition that Integrative Meta-perspective draws on the whole of intelligence even more explicitly gets at this result. Later we will see how intelligence's

---

mechanistic. Later in the century, several key systems contributors, most notably Gregory Bateson and Humberto Maturana, in different ways again placed the challenge of thinking of living systems in living terms forefront in their thinking. But while their formulations added important further insight, as with the ideas of von Bertalanffy, they remained yet short of providing more than general principles.

various aspects reflect different relationships of difference and connectedness and also help us understand particular aspects of the world's
apples-and-oranges complexity.

By drawing consciously on human sensibility's whole-box-of crayons
multiplicity, Integrative Meta-perspective provides a direct response to
von Bertalanffy's insightful framing of the systemic task. It makes it
possible to think about living systems in living terms. And more than
just this, it makes it possible to think in ways that honor the particular
kind of life we are by virtue of being human.

Today we can find systems language being used to describe ideas
that in various ways extend both the past's heroic and romantic traditions. It is important to appreciate when this is the case, given that the
results necessarily leave us short. And the fact that such notions often
have the potential to lead us badly astray makes this kind of awareness
doubly important.[10]

The phrase "systems science" is often used to describe the heroic-
tradition approaches that have given us the digital and genetic revolu-
tions. While such approaches have produced significant advances, we
need to recognize that the kind of thinking they reflect is different fundamentally from the kind of systems ideas we have interest in. Indeed,
extending such thinking to extremes can result in particularly silly and
often decidedly dangerous conclusions. I think in particular of techno-
utopian thought—beliefs that in effect deify the technological and assume that new inventions will solve all our problems. Later, I will describe how some of the circumstances with the greatest potential to be
the end of us as a species are products of techno-utopian assumptions.

From the other, more archetypally feminine/romantic tradition
side of things, we find several related traps. People can equate systems thinking with spiritual ideas, most commonly with notions from

---

10 The awkward, in-between place we too often reside in today with Cultural
   Maturity's changes further adds to the importance of this kind of recognition. Because thinking that has its roots in the past's heroic and romantic traditions protects us from the more demanding, whole-box-of-crayons
   kind of understanding that comes with Integrative Meta-perspective, people in our time can find it more attractive, not less. This that might seem a
   paradoxical reaction makes it even more important that we know just what
   makes culturally mature understanding different—and essential.

Eastern philosophy, such as Buddhist or Taoist teachings, or with the more nature-centered spiritual beliefs of tribal societies. We can also find systems thinking confused with more liberal/humanist belief, with its emphasis on our shared humanity and actions that benefit the less fortunate.

Again, while such thinking can provide value, it is wholly different from our concern. And in a similar way, when extended to an extreme, it can become silly, and if not so obviously dangerous, certainly a bit delusional. We see this kind of result with the trivialness of New Age thought and the easy ardencies of the more extreme and ideological of populist political positions. Commonly such thinking only ends up demonizing more right-hand sensibilities in the name of truth. And even when it gets beyond the worst of traps, it is vulnerable to being used as an excuse for a particularly debilitating kind of cynicism and fatalism. We find some of the most extreme of both utopian and dystopian thinking in people who fall for this kind of systemic misconception.

Seen from the vantage of Integrative Meta-perspective, these two "systems" traditions can just as accurately be thought of as systems thinking's opposite. Throughout the book I will return to a radically significant observation that supports this conclusion more conceptually. It turns out that polarity at its most fundamental juxtaposes not two contrasting kinds of difference, as we tend to assume, but rather difference on one hand juxtaposed with unity on the other.[11] Ways of thinking that come out of the modern age heroic tradition in the end identify with difference. Ways of thinking that come out of the modern age romantic tradition in the end identify with unity. Understood in this way, each of these two "systems" traditions specifically takes sides, and does so in a quite ultimate sense. And just adding these contrasting traditions together in some kind of compromise ultimately gets us no closer. Thus, each not only leaves us short of where we need to go, it could not do so more absolutely.

A key additional observation helps further highlight how what we are dealing with is fundamentally new. I will draw on it frequently in chapters ahead as we apply Integrative Meta-perspective to specific

---

11 Chapter Three addresses the conceptual basis for this observation.

cultural challenges. One of the defining characteristics of culturally mature thought is that while it increases our appreciation for connectedness, it also increases our appreciation for *real* difference. (I emphasize the word "real" to distinguish perceptions of difference based on projection—the kind that gives us bigotry and absolutist ideologies—from an appreciation of ways different aspects of systems are authentically different.) That both of these results would be seen simultaneously makes no sense if we are limited to usual ways to thinking. From Integrative Meta-perspective's more whole-box-of-crayons systemic vantage, it is just how things work.

"Bridging" Polarities and Understanding a Newly Necessary Completeness

For me, the way Integrative Meta-perspective makes it newly possible to think about living systems in more life-acknowledging—and human life-acknowledging—ways, provides the most precise frame for understanding how Integrative Meta-perspective is new and distinguishing it from other ways of thinking. Later we shall see how, given that Integrative Meta-perspective is about understanding more generally, it ultimately provides a new, more dynamic and generative picture whatever we wish to understand, even if our focus is the simply physical.[12] But this particularly conceptual way of thinking about what becomes different is only one strategy. An approach I used early on in my efforts to articulate where Cultural Maturity's changes take us introduces another that, if fully understood, provides an important practical tool for making needed distinctions.

In first developing Creative Systems Theory, I would often speak about how culturally mature understanding "bridges" the polar assumptions of times past. The notion at least makes a good starting point for thinking about needed changes. And a conundrum I encountered in trying to make it work adds to understanding by shedding further light on the challenges of articulation.

Our human tendency to think in the language of polarity manifests not just with issues where we tend to take sides, but pretty much wherever we

---

12 See Chapter Six.

look. Most philosophical thought has been dualistic. Medicine, certainly in modern times, has tended to place mind and body in separate worlds. And the conclusions of science and religion, for most people, reside in wholly distinct realities. In the next chapter, we will look at how understanding throughout history has been based on evolving juxtapositions of more archetypally masculine and archetypally feminine values and ways of thinking.

One of the most defining characteristics of major conceptual advances of the last century is how often they created links—bridges, if you will—between categories of thought that we had previously kept separate, indeed, that we have often considered opposites. We witness this phenomenon, for example, with both matter and energy and space and time in physics, with humankind and nature in the best of thinking in the biological sciences, and with conscious and unconscious in modern psychology's new formulations. I organized the whole of my second book, *Necessary Wisdom*, around this important recognition.

But while framing Cultural Maturity's changes in terms of the "bridging" of past polar assumptions provided an adequate shorthand early on in my work, this approach ultimately proved less helpful than I had hoped. I found that unless a person's thinking already included at least the beginnings of culturally mature perspective, as often as not, speaking in this way would result in missing the point entirely. People would tend to assume that bridging meant the same as joining or averaging. The Dilemma of Representation again reared its ugly head.

In an effort to make the concept more useful, I began to put the word "bridging" in quotes. I also drew increasingly on an image that expands on my earlier reference to how engaging Cultural Maturity's changes is like stepping over a threshold: an archway marking entry into Cultural Maturity's new territory. Polarity in the image is represented by the archway's columns. To help get beyond the Dilemma of Representation, I applied the image in a way that draws on some visual sleight of hand. "Bridging" as we might customarily use the term would involve joining the archway's columns (and the contrasting archetypally masculine and archetypally feminine qualities they represent). But the kind of "bridging" that comes with Integrative Meta-perspective reflects something wholly different. It involves proceeding through the archway and into the territory beyond.

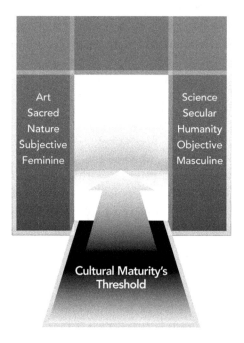

Fig. 2-2. "Bridging" Conceptual Polarities

I also made increasing use of a further CST notion—the concept of polar fallacies. CST delineates three different ways that we can miss the mark in our attempts to get beyond polarized thinking. We can fall off the right-hand, more archetypally masculine side of the road; we can fall off the left-hand, more archetypally feminine side of the road; or we can walk down the white line in the middle (and get hit by cars going both ways). The theory calls these various ways of stopping short of culturally mature systemic understanding Separation Fallacies, Unity Fallacies, and Compromise Fallacies.[13] The

---

13 The more elaborated definitions below are excerpted from *Cultural Maturity:*

"Separation Fallacies equate truth with difference—with perceived fundamental distinctions such as between men and women, the material

language brings us back to my earlier observation that polarity at its most basic contrasts difference with unity. I concluded each chapter in *Necessary Wisdom* by listing Separation, Unity, and Compromise Fallacies pertinent to that chapter's topic.

---

and the spiritual, the intellect and the emotions. And they give greatest value to the more right-hand, archetypally masculine side of the pertinent polarity (here, men, the material, and the intellect.) Some common Separation Fallacies: We are each wholly unique, individual. Experts have the answers. Final truth is what can be rationally articulated and objectively demonstrated. Man is wholly separate from nature and has rightful dominion over her. Change is a simple product of cause and effect.

"In contrast, Unity Fallacies identify with connectedness. They give greatest value to the more left-hand, archetypally feminine side of any polarity. Related Unity Fallacies might include: In the end, we are all one (differences are ultimately irrelevant). The ordinary person knows best (better than leaders and institutions). Final truth is what we know from within. The task is to always live in accord with nature. Everything happens for a reason, even if that reason remains mysterious (it is all connected). Unity Fallacies argue against distinction and emphasize oneness. They may claim a transcendence of polarity, but in fact they very specifically take sides. They give their allegiance to the softer, more creatively germinal hand of creation—to the spiritual over the material, feelings over facts, the timeless over the specific.

"And Compromise Fallacies split the difference. They confuse averaging with mature systemic perspective. A few related Compromise Fallacies are: We are all different in our own ways ("different strokes for different folks"). Good decisions come from everybody having an equal say. There are lots of kinds of truth and each has its merits. Nature can be different things to different people. In the end, life is what we make of it. Some Compromise Fallacies advocate a safe additive middle ground. Others argue correctly for multiple options, but give us nothing to help us beyond this accurate but meager observation—they claim to address diversity but fail to address what makes differences different. Compromise fallacies take us beyond black and white, but in the end replace it only with shades of gray."

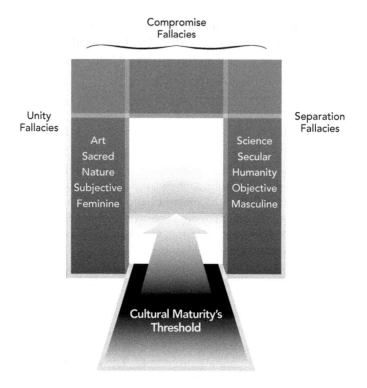

Fig. 2-3. "Bridging" and Polar Fallacies

Because confusions have too often persisted in spite of my best efforts at clarification, over time, I've come to use the language of "bridging" much less often. The Dilemma of Representation can be remarkably impervious to explanation (further evidence for the fact that we are dealing not just with beliefs, but with patterns of cognitive organization). When I need a metaphor now, more often I will draw on the box-of-crayons image.

The box-of-crayons metaphor doesn't wholly escape the Dilemma of Representation (such is the Dilemma's necessary hold). For example, the various hues can still be added or averaged, even if the result would often be a less-than-appealing muddy brown. But the box communicates the stepping back that provides Integrative Meta-perspective's overarching vantage in a way that the simple notion of "bridging" does not. And the image comes closer to capturing how Integrative Meta-perspective increases our appreciation at once for interrelationship and for difference.

The contrasting hues of the various crayons help highlight how we are dealing not just with interconnections between aspects, but with apples-and-oranges differences that become not diminished, but in fact more distinct, with Integrative Meta-perspective.

An observation that follows from these reflections helps bring them together in a particularly striking way. It concerns what it means to be "objective." I've spoken of Integrative Meta-perspective making understanding more complete. It is important to appreciate that I don't mean complete in some sense of finished. Rather, I've used the word simply to acknowledge that such perspective takes more into account. But the fact that the "more" that is taken into account better includes the whole of who we are, however imperfectly it may do so, is of no small significance.

Modern age thought has equated completeness with objectivity. But from the vantage of culturally mature perspective, this was, in fact, objectivity of a most preliminary and limited sort. Besides leaving culture's parental status untouched, it left experience as a whole divided—objective opposed to subjective, mind opposed to body, thoughts opposed to feelings (and anything else that does not conform to modernity's rationalist/materialist worldview).

In one sense, Integrative Meta-perspective is less "objective" than what it replaces—being that it draws on aspects of intelligence that before gave us the more subjective parts of experience. But equally well we could argue that it is more objective, if by "objective" we mean better able to grasp all that is involved. We cannot ultimately claim to be objective if we have left out much of the evidence.

Cultural Maturity as a Species "Growing Up"

I've made reference to how the changes that produce Integrative Meta-perspective find parallels with second-half-of-life changes in our personal development. Drawing on those parallels provides support of a more visceral sort for this chapter's often abstract conceptual reflections.[14]

---

14 While making analogy with personal maturity provides important insight for understanding Cultural Maturity, it is true too that personal maturity and Cultural Maturity have key differences and we can get into trouble in our thinking if we don't recognize them. In *Cultural Maturity:*

I concluded the previous chapter by linking challenges that could be the end of us to themes that cut through needed new skills and sensibilities: getting beyond mythologized, chosen-people/evil-other beliefs; realizing a new maturity in our relationship to limits; and applying more systemic measures in all parts of our lives (and in particular to how we think about wealth and progress). Each of these themes manifests in more circumscribed ways with second-half-of-life maturity in our personal lives. Taking a moment to reflect on just how they do helps further fill out where Integrative Meta-perspective takes us.

Getting Beyond Us-Versus-Them Beliefs

We've seen how Integrative Meta-perspective helps us better recognize projection and get beyond the "single crayon" ideological easy answers of times past—whether on the global stage, between social groups, or between those who ascribe to differing belief systems. A related kind of change, but of a more limited sort, is an essential aspect of personal maturity.

This is not always what we see in a person's later years. If a person fails to take on the requisite developmental challenges, we can just as easily find a solidifying of ideological beliefs, a "hardening of the categories." But if second-half-of-life developmental tasks are successfully engaged, they bring a greater capacity for perspective. Projection and polarized thinking tend to lessen considerably. At the very least, personal maturity tends to make one more able to appreciate that issues tend to be more complex than we at first might assume.

In times past, this capacity has not been an option at a cultural level. But it has also not been necessary. Indeed, chosen-people/evil-other assumptions have always before been necessary to the effective functioning of societies. But as we have seen, today the opposite has become the case. Without a critical mass of people capable of the needed perspective at a species level, the result will be countries with ever more dysfunctional governments and no reason not to use their stockpiles of ever more lethal weaponry.

A *Guidebook for the Future*, I both fill out the parallels and tease apart the important differences.

The Fact of Real Limits

I've described how systemically partial views, by their nature, hide myths of limitlessness. And I've emphasized how culturally mature understanding makes real limits not just more easily recognized but something we can embrace. From Integrative Meta-perspective's more whole-box-of-crayons systemic vantage, we better appreciate how limits are inherent to how things work.

Again we find a similar but more limited kind of recognition with personal development. Indeed, it could be argued that it is limits that most explicitly mark the challenges of second-half-of-life maturity in our individual lives. Certainly, it is limits that tend to first intrude on our attention. As we get older, we confront that real limits exist both to our physical strength and to our bodily beauty. And ultimately we face life's most ultimate limit, the fact of our mortality. In giving up youth's dreams of ultimate possibility, we find in their place the ability to see things more accurately, and more wisely.

This kind of recognition has similarly not before been necessary, nor has it been an option, at a cultural level. I've described how the belief that in the end there are no limits has been central to both heroic and romantic narratives. Today, the need to acknowledge real limits is commonly the task that first makes its presence felt with the challenges of Cultural Maturity. It is also what may most make the necessity of Cultural Maturity's changes inescapable. Climate change and the extinction of the planet's species, for example, represent at once some of our time's greatest dangers and the phenomena that may have the greatest potential to open our eyes to what is needed. Put in the language of educators, it is the fact of real limits that may most serve to make our time a "teachable moment."

A Crisis of Narrative and of Human Purpose

I've given particular emphasis to how any definition of progress that can result in real human advancement must be more systemic. It must better include the full complexity of ingredients that bring meaning to our lives. Integrative Meta-perspective, by better incorporating all of the ways that we engage experience, makes a more whole-box-of-crayons definition of progress feel like common sense.

The need for a related kind of evolution of narrative and rethinking of meaning confronts us as we reach personal maturity. Later we will

examine more conceptually how what we observe in personal development with the common phenomenon of a "midlife crisis" has important parallels with what I have described with our modern Crisis of
Purpose. In each case, we are attempting to take heroic and romantic
stories beyond their usefulness—in individual development, such stories as they define the tasks of young adulthood; in culture, as they have
manifested with modern age narrative.

Wisdom in an individual life is about using a more systemic and
complete appreciation for what most matters as our referent. Integrative Meta-perspective offers a related, more systemic and complete
picture of significance for the human story as a whole. Our future well-
being depends on it.

CHAPTER THREE

Rethinking Intelligence— Understanding's Multiplicity and Its Creative Consequences

The observation that intelligence has multiple aspects is both more fundamental in its significance and more radical in its implications than might immediately be apparent. This chapter addresses a small handful of intelligence-related observations that are particularly pertinent to understanding Integrative Meta-perspective and what it asks of us.

We will look first at how the way our multiple intelligences work together provides essential insight into what ultimately makes us human. We will then examine how the picture that results helps us make sense of why, in times past, we've tended to think in the language of polarity—in terms of us-versus-them juxtapositions and interplaying opposites more generally. Finally, we will turn to how an appreciation for intelligence's larger complexity further clarifies what defines our time in the human story and how the implications of Integrative Meta-perspective differ from more familiar ways of thinking about the future.

Because the ideas we will examine with this chapter necessarily draw on intelligence's multiple aspects with particular depth, making sense of them will require at least the beginnings of Integrative Meta-perspective. In turn, taking time with these notions will help fill out our understanding of what entry into Cultural Maturity's new territory of experience requires in some particularly significant ways.[1]

---

1   The basic notions in this chapter about intelligence, polarity, and contrasting ways of thinking about the future can all be found in more elaborated

The Fact of Multiple Intelligences

The fact that Integrative Meta-perspective involves consciously drawing on more aspects of intelligence—more of our diverse ways of knowing—than we've traditionally been able to make use of at one time is arguably the best way to think about its mechanisms. Mature systemic perspective applies intelligence in the rational sense. Indeed, it offers that we do so with new precision. But, at the same time, it draws deeply on emotional intelligence, the part of human sensibility that gives affective color to our lives and in particular informs our relationships with others. It also provides more conscious access to the imaginal intelligence of metaphor, myth, dreams, and the artistic. And it helps us connect more deeply with the intelligence of the body, the kind of knowing that comes alive though the senses, that allows us to engage the erotic, and that most affirms our relatedness with nature.

The fact that intelligence has multiple aspects also provides one of the best ways to begin to grasp how Integrative Meta-perspective produces the kind of understanding that it does. Because each aspect of intelligence has an essential role in making us human, each necessarily has a voice in the life-affirming, and specifically human life-affirming, kind of systemic thinking that will be increasingly essential to addressing challenges before us as a species.

We find support for the central significance of intelligence's multiplicity in the parallels between personal maturity and Cultural Maturity that I drew on in the previous chapter. I've noted how the best of thinking in our later years applies not just knowledge, but also wisdom. Knowledge can be articulated quite well by the intellect alone. Wisdom, in contrast, requires a more fully encompassing kind of intelligence, one that draws on all of who we are. Wisdom results not just because we better include all the aspects of our questions, but also because, when seeking answers, we don't leave out essential parts of ourselves.

It is reasonable to ask just why we have multiple intelligences in the first place. Given that our various intelligences work in such different ways and often provide contradictory kinds of information, the answer is not at all obvious. Creative Systems Theory proposes that the explanation is directly pertinent to the answer of an even more fundamental question: What is it that makes us particular, if not unique, as a species?

---

form in my lengthy book *Cultural Maturity: A Guidebook for the Future*.

People have proposed multiple legitimate candidates. There is the fact that we stand upright, letting us look out over our worlds—which is at least unusual. The fact that we communicate not just with sounds, but with pictures and words is more obviously consequential. There is also the complexity of our social structures, how we organize ourselves not just into bands and flocks, but into villages and nations.

CST affirms the validity of each of these explanations. But it also proposes that there is something more basic, a characteristic that arguably underlies each of them. What makes us particular as a species is the richness and complexity of our tool-making prowess. We are makers not just of things, but also of belief systems. And we are makers of meaning.

The theory frames this conclusion more conceptually by observing that what makes us particular is the depth and audacity of our "creative" capacities, using the word "creative" in a particularly encompassing sense. Here the term applies to the scientific and technical as much as it does the artistic. And it concerns the everyday and practical just as much as the new and innovative. It refers to the fact that we are generative beings, able to consciously craft our realities, often in strikingly innovative ways.

In his book *Sapiens, a Brief History of Humankind*, Yuval Noah Harari similarly emphasizes our tool-making abilities and begins to make the needed link to intelligence's multiplicity. In his words, "Homo sapiens rules the world because it is the only animal that can believe in things that exist purely in its own imagination, such as gods, states, money and human rights."[2] CST lets us be more precise in making the link. It describes how human intelligence is specifically structured to support our tool-making, meaning-making natures. It proposes that we are the unique creatures we are not just because we are conscious, but because of the specific ways the various aspects of our intelligence work together. Human intelligence is uniquely configured to support creative change and the kind of understanding necessary to make one's way creatively in the world.[3]

---

2 Yuval Noah Harari, *Sapiens, a Brief History of Humankind*, 2014, Vintage.

3 In Chapter Six, I will propose that the notion that intelligence (and thus how we see the world) is creatively ordered has major significance in the history of ideas. It invites us to entertain a new, more dynamic and en-

I've observed that we can think of intelligence's various aspects as the crayons in the systemic box. CST goes further and puts this picture in motion—and a specifically creative kind of motion. It describes how our various intelligences—or we might say "sensibilities," to better reflect all they encompass—relate in ways that are inherently generative.

The theory delineates how different ways of knowing, and different relationships between ways of knowing, predominate at specific times in any human change process and function together as creativity's mechanism. Think of our various modes of intelligence as not just static crayons in a box, but dynamically juxtaposed like colors on a color wheel. That wheel, like the wheel of a car or a Ferris wheel, is continually turning, continually in motion. The way the various facets of intelligence relate one to another makes change, and specifically purposeful change, inherent to our natures.

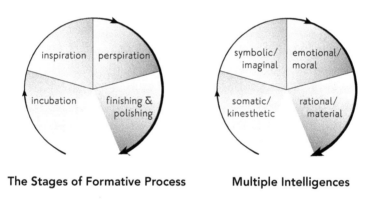

The Stages of Formative Process   Multiple Intelligences

Fig. 3-1. Formative Process and Intelligence

The diagram in Fig 3-1 depicts how CST links the workings of intelligence and the stages of formative process. In other writings, I clarify how each creative stage in some way draws on each kind of intelligence.[4] But it is also the case that one kind of intelligence is most defining at each stage.

compassing Fundamental Organizing Concept to replace the modern age notion that reality is, in the end, a great machine.

4 See *The Creative Imperative: Human Growth and Planetary Evolution, Cultural Maturity: A Guidebook for the Future*, or CSTHome.org.

CST identifies four basic types of intelligence. The theory uses fancier language (see Fig 3-1), but for ease of conversation, we can refer to them simply as I have here—rational intelligence, emotional intelligence, imaginal intelligence, and body intelligence. CST proposes that these different ways of knowing represent not just diverse approaches to processing information, but the windows through which we make sense of our worlds. More than this, they reflect the formative tendencies that lead us to shape our worlds in the ways that we do.

A brief look at a single creative process helps bring these relationships to life. I've often done sculpture in stone. When I work on a piece of stone, the creative process proceeds through a progression of creative stages and associated sensibilities. Creative processes unfold in varied ways, but the following outline is generally representative:

Creative "Incubation" and Body Intelligence: Before formally getting started on a piece of sculpture, my sense of where it will go is murky at best. Creative processes begin in darkness. I am aware of a certain felt sense that I want to communicate, but I have only the most beginning sense of how I will proceed or where proceeding will take me.

This is creativity's "incubation" stage. The dominant intelligence here is the kinesthetic, body intelligence, if you will. It is like I am pregnant, but don't quite yet know with what. What I do know takes the form of "inklings" and faint "glimmerings," inner sensings. If I want to feed this part of the creative process, I do things that help me to be reflective and to connect in my body.

Creative "Inspiration" and Imaginal Intelligence: Generativity's second stage propels the new thing created out of darkness into first light. As I work with the stone, I begin to have "ahas." My mind floods with images and possible approaches for expression. Some of these first insights take the form of thoughts. Others manifest more as metaphors or expressive gestures.

In this "inspiration" stage, the dominant intelligence is the imaginal—that which most defines myth, the let's-pretend world of young children, and the language of dreams. The products of this period in the creative process may appear suddenly—Archimedes's "eureka"—or they may come more subtly and gradually. It is this stage, and this part of our larger sensibility, that we tend to most traditionally associate with things creative.

Creative "Perspiration" and Emotional Intelligence: With the next stage in formative process, we leave behind the realm of first possibilities and move into the world of manifest form. With the piece of sculpture, I try out specific approaches. And I get down to the hard work of shaping and crafting. This is creation's "perspiration" stage.

The dominant intelligence here is different still, more emotional and visceral—the intelligence of heart and guts. It is at this stage that I confront the hard work of finding just the right approach and the most satisfying means of expression. I also confront limits to my skills and am challenged to push beyond them. The perspiration stage tends to bring a new moral commitment and emotional edginess. I must compassionately, but unswervingly, confront what I have created if it is to stand the test of time.

Creative "Finishing and Polishing" and Rational Intelligence: Generativity's fourth stage is more concerned with detail and refinement. The sculpture's basic form is now established, but much yet remains to do. My attention now turns to the work's surfaces, and to stepping back to be sure there is nothing I have forgotten.

Rational intelligence orders this "finishing and polishing" stage. This period is more conscious and more concerned with aesthetic precision than the periods previous. It is also more concerned with audience and outcome. It brings final focus to the creative work, and offers the clarity of thought and nuances of style needed for effective communication.

CST applies this relationship between intelligence and formative process to the workings of human experience as a whole. It proposes that the same general progression of sensibilities we see with a creative project orders creative growth in every kind of human system. It argues that we see similar patterns at all levels—from the psychological development of an individual, to the growth of a relationship, to the development of an organization. And of particular importance for this inquiry, it proposes that a related kind of patterning orders culture and its evolution.

A few snapshots: The same bodily intelligence that orders creative "incubation" plays a particularly prominent role in the infant's rhythmic world of movement, touch, and taste. The realities of early tribal cultures also draw deeply on body sensibilities. Truth in tribal societies is synonymous with the rhythms of nature and, through dance, song, story, and drumbeat, with the body of the tribe.

The same imaginal intelligence that we saw ordering creative "inspiration" takes prominence in the play-centered world of the young child. We also hear its voice with particular strength in early civilizations—such as in ancient Greece or Egypt, with the Incas and Aztecs in the Americas, or in the classical East—with their mythic pantheons and great symbolic tales.

The same emotional intelligence that orders creative "perspiration" tends to occupy center stage in adolescence, with its deepening passions and pivotal struggles for identity. It can be felt with particular strength also in the beliefs and values of the European Middle Ages, times marked by feudal struggle and ardent moral conviction (and, today, in places such as the Middle East where struggle and conflict seem to be forever recurring).

The same rational intelligence that comes forward with the "finishing and polishing" tasks of creativity takes new prominence in young adulthood, as we strive to create our unique place in the world of adult expectations. This more refined and refining aspect of intelligence stepped to the fore culturally with the Renaissance and the Age of Reason and, in the West, has held sway into modern times.

The Fact of Polarity

We are not done with intelligence and will return shortly for some essential additions to this creative picture. But what I have described invites conjecture with regard to another question that first deserves our attention. I've observed how in times past we've tended to think in the language of polarity. As with intelligence's multiplicity, we reasonably ask just why this has been the case.

I've suggested an important part of the explanation. Thinking in polar terms has helped simplify experience and make it something we can tolerate. The more black-and-white picture that results makes what might otherwise seem like overwhelming complexity feel more manageable. And the ideological absolutes that tend to accompany polarized thinking similarly protect us from intrusion by life's all too common uncertainties.

But polarity's ubiquity in human understanding suggests that something more interesting is at work. CST describes how polarity is fundamental to how we think. And it goes further to propose that the answer to the question of why we tend to think in the language of polarity is the same as the answer I have just suggested for why we have multiple intelligences. Polarity, in a similar way, follows directly from our tool-making, meaning making, we could say simply "creative" natures. We got a hint of this creative significance with my earlier observation that polarities of all sorts juxtapose qualities/tendencies that are more archetypally masculine with qualities/tendencies of a more archetypally feminine sort. The gender-linked language suggests a relationship that is in some way "procreative."

In introducing a creative frame, I often make polarity rather than the fact of intelligence's multiplicity my starting point. In a similar way to what we saw for intelligence, CST lets us map polarity's creative workings. The theory delineates how a predictable sequence of polar dynamics organizes experience over the course of any human creative/ formative process (see Figure 3-2).

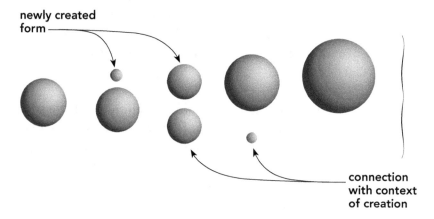

newly created
form

connection
with context
of creation

Fig. 3-2. Creative Differentiation

A brief description: Any human formative/creative process begins in an original unity. We can think of this original unity equally well in terms of the wholeness of the already known or in terms of the mystery that necessarily precedes the appearance of new form. Polarity first appears with initial insights and the budding off of fresh possibility. Polarity at this point is necessarily yet fragile, but it also imbues experience with the magic and wonder of the just born. Over time, the newly created form pushes away from its beginnings, becoming in the process more solidly established. With this pushing away, polarity too becomes more solid and established. Eventually, the task shifts more to that of finishing and detail. The newly completed object increasingly now takes center stage, and attention moves even further away from creation's original context.

As we saw with intelligence's multiplicity, this sequence plays out not just with creative dynamics of the more everyday tool-making sort. CST delineates how polarity predictably follows this same creative progression with every kind of human creative/formative process, including individual psychological development, how human relationships grow over time, the growth of organizations, and of particular pertinence for these reflections, the evolution of culture.

Applying a creative frame to the workings of polarity assists us most immediately by helping us begin to appreciate how polar dynamics can shape experience in different ways at different times and places. But it also helps us begin to address a further critical question: How is it that today we are beginning to think in ways that "bridge" the polarized and polarizing assumptions of times past? Put more specifically in terms of the topic of this book, how it is that Integrative Meta-perspective's more complete picture is something that we might expect to encounter?

For the answer to make sense, we need first to recognize that my descriptions of formative/creative process thus far have gotten us only part of the way. We could call what I have delineated to this point creative process' "differentiation phase." Additional stages that we can miss if we focus only on the object being created are essential to how formative processes work. Differentiation describes only part of what makes a process creative. Just as important are more integrative dynamics.

Creativity's "integration phase" forms a complement to the more difference-generating dynamics of Creative Differentiation—a second half to the creative process. It varies greatly in length and intensity. With it the finished form reconnects with the creative context from which it arose, both past forms from which it pushed away to become something separate and the organizational realities in ourselves from which it was born. We can think of it as formative process' time of seasoning or ripening.

Creative Integration fundamentally reorders experience. With a simple creative act like working on a piece of sculpture, we are able step back from our effort and appreciate it with a new, more encompassing kind of perspective. In doing so, we become better able to recognize the relationship of one part to another. We also better appreciate the relationship of the work to its creative contexts, to ourselves and to the time and place in which it was created. We have common everyday language for this important result. What before seemed wholly new and distinct becomes "second nature."

We recognize something similar with second-half-of-life challenges in our personal development. The tasks of young adulthood focus on achievement and the delineation of identity. With life's second half, the important tasks have more to do with perspective and with right relationship—with ourselves, with the people in our lives, and in the end, with life's important questions. Existence becomes more complete and at the same time in essential ways more ordinary. We become better able to see just what is.

These further stages become particularly significant if our interest lies with the specific challenges of our time. CST delineates how the "growing up" on which our future depends is a product of this specifically integrative kind of dynamic. When I've spoken of how we experience the result with Integrative Meta-perspective as a "new common sense," I've been making reference not just to the fact that its more sophisticated vantage is developmentally timely, but also to how it reflects such "second nature" dynamics. The newly created thing that becomes second nature in this case is the human endeavor as a whole. Today we confront the need to hold reality in more integrative, whole-box-of-crayons ways in every part of our personal and collective lives.

The diagram below, what CST calls the Creative Function, maps the progression of creative process, including these necessary integrative dynamics. The Creative Function lies at the heart of CST's formulations.[5]

---

5 See *The Creative Imperative: Human Growth and Planetary Evolution* or *Cultural Maturity: A Guidebook for the Future* for more detailed looks at the Creative Function and its implications.

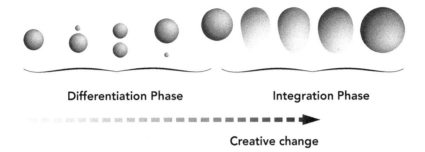

Differentiation Phase   Integration Phase

Creative change

Fig. 3-3. The Creative Function

The Creative Function helps clarify and fill out a couple of previous polarity-related observations. The first concerns the way I have described polarity as having more archetypally feminine and more archetypally masculine qualities. When polarity is framed creatively, we find the more archetypally feminine half of polarity with the more creatively germinal side of any stage-specific juxtaposition (in this representation, with the lower pole of each stage[6]). We find the more archetypally masculine half of polarity with the more creatively manifest side of any stage-specific juxtaposition (in this representation, with the upper pole of each stage). This recognition will take on particular importance later in this chapter when we look at some of the implications of how the relationship between the archetypally feminine and the archetypally masculine evolves over time.

The Creative Function also supports and adds important detail to my earlier observation that polarity at its most basic juxtaposes difference/distinction on one hand with unity/connectedness on the other. We can think of the Creative Function as a map of the various ways

---

6 CST describes how some polarities manifest in ways that are more vertical (think of being more in one's head versus more in one's feelings), and others in ways that are more horizontal (think of more expressive versus more receptive sensibilities). With more horizontal juxtapositions, we find the more archetypally feminine half of polarity with the inner aspect of any stage-specific juxtaposition, the more archetypally masculine with more outer aspects.

that more difference-identifying and more unity-identifying beliefs manifest and relate to one another over time. Difference-related beliefs correspond to the half of any polar juxtaposition that reflects the evolving solidification of form. Unity-related beliefs correspond to the half of any polarity that ties most directly to origin and context.

Creative Integration and Intelligence

I've promised to return for some necessary additions to intelligence's creative picture. This more elaborated mapping of polarity's workings alerts us to the fact that previous intelligence-related descriptions are not yet complete. Previously I've described how our relationship to intelligence's multiplicity evolves over the first half of any formative process, proceeding from bodily intelligence's primacy with creative incubation to rationality's preeminence with formative process' finishing and polishing stage. But this look at the workings of polarity makes clear that intelligence's changes don't stop with finishing and polishing. Intelligence's story has more to teach us.

Our relationship to intelligence continues to evolve over the course of the second half of any creative/formative process. Consistent with what we saw with polarity, it does so in ways that both provide perspective and are increasingly integrative. We caught a glimpse of this result with Chapter Two's introduction to Cultural Maturity's cognitive changes. I observed how a more conscious and specifically integrative kind of intelligence orders the unique developmental capacities, the wisdom, of a lifetime's second half. I also observed how a related, more encompassing relationship to intelligence's multiplicity at a cultural level is central to the mechanisms of Integrative Meta-perspective.

CST adds essential nuance. It describes how Integrative Meta-perspective makes it possible to apply our intelligences in various combinations and balances as time and situation warrant. Integrative Meta-perspective is about a growing ability not just to engage the work as a whole, but to draw on ourselves as a whole in relationship to it.

Conceptual advances of the last century support this more integrative picture of intelligence's workings. With a good many of them, we find at least implied not just a more systemic grasp of the relationship between polar opposites, but a more encompassing engagement with intelligence's multiplicity. I think of how we find metaphorical references to mystery and the mythic in the language of modern physics—black holes, quarks and quasars, white dwarfs. There is also how biology has gradually become more than just an arm's-length study, how it has come to better acknowledge our commonality with other species and today accept an almost sacred responsibility for the well-being of life as a whole. The importance of a more encompassing picture of intelligence is most explicit with psychology and psychiatry. People are most familiar with how Sigmund Freud gave new attention to unconscious forces, but an evolving deeper appreciation of intelligence's multiple aspects has been a centrally significant part of advances over the last century.[7]

We associate the Age of Reason with Descartes's assertion that "I think, therefore I am." We could make a parallel assertion for each of the other cultural stages: "I am embodied, therefore I am"; "I imagine, therefore I am"; "I am a moral being, therefore I am"; and, if the concept of Cultural Maturity is accurate, "I understand maturely and systemically—with the whole of myself—therefore I am." CST proposes that this chapter's reflections about the creative workings of intelligence and polarity become possible because such consciously integrative dynamics are today reordering how we think and perceive.[8]

---

7 A series of influential thinkers contributed to the more encompassing picture of intelligence that I have drawn on here. These include Carl Jung, with his special emphasis on the mythic and imaginal dimensions of intelligence; Wilhelm Reich, with his focus on the intelligence of the body; Harry Stack Sullivan and later humanistic thinkers such a Carl Rogers, with their fresh thinking about human relationships and emotional functioning; and transpersonal contributors such as Abraham Maslow, who brought new attention to exceptional capacities and the spiritual dimension.

8 I apply a creative picture of intelligence's workings not just to the content of what I write, but also to the writing itself. Marshall McLuhan famously pronounced that "the medium is the message." If culturally mature writing is to work, the medium must at least be consistent with the message. Toward this end, as you can see with my frequent use of metaphors and references to bodily experience, I draw more extensively on intelligence's multiplicity than a person might expect with expression that is so often theoretical. The whole of intelligence is needed to fully grasp any culturally

Developmental Amnesias, Transition, and the Dilemma of Trajectory

We need some additional intelligence- and polarity-related recognitions if we are to fully appreciate the implications of this chapter's reflections. Each provides important further conceptual insights and also introduces language that proves powerful when we are addressing challenges ahead for us as a species.

The first recognition concerns an important question that we could easily neglect to ask: Just why is the more integrative picture that we find with Cultural Maturity's cognitive changes anything new? To understand why this is a question at all, we need to look more closely at previous cultural stages. The modern age picture, for example—with rationality standing alone as intelligence's last word and truth manifesting as juxtaposed objective and subjective worlds—might seem the obvious result from what I have described. But this is not the only possibility or even the one we might most reasonably expect. If each new chapter in culture's evolution had simply added a further layer to understanding—with each layer combining with those before—modern age thought would have already succeeded with the integrative task.

For the picture I have described to make sense, we need an additional insight that follows from how creative processes work. Creative processes involve amnesias, necessary forgettings between stages so that we don't fall back into the safety of more familiar realities. Such creative amnesias are familiar from personal development. We recognize them in how difficult it can be for adolescents to make sense of the behavior of young children even though they themselves were children only a few years before.

---

mature concept, and certainly it is needed if a person is to make sense of CST's highly delineated patterning concepts.

This matching of medium with message also manifests in the causalities implied in how I often structure sentences. Traditional prose tends to obey the laws of more right-hand, simple cause-and-effect causality. Poetry, in drawing most strongly on non-rational aspects of intelligence, as often applies causality of a more left-hand, tautological sort—"a rose is a rose." I draw on a bit of both and also often extend beyond them to apply a more explicitly "creative" sort of causality. Every CST concept reflects causality of this more dynamic, systemic sort.

Later, we witness them in the way young adults can find the behavior of adolescents totally baffling. CST proposes that it is because of such necessary forgettings that in modern times we've lost any depth of access to pre-rational intelligences and polarity's more germinal manifestations.[9]

This recognition of developmental amnesias helps us in a couple of key ways. It provides further confirmation that Integrative Meta-perspective engages us in a kind of process that is new in the human experience. And it also does something else that is essential to understanding what our times ask of us. It highlights the fact that much has been lost as well as gained in culture's story to this point. The mechanisms that have allowed culture to evolve have also required that important aspects of who we are be left behind.

Precisely because of those amnesias, we can easily miss that anything has been lost. But the implications are significant. At the least, developmental amnesias necessarily leave us with a distorted and impoverished understanding of history. Much that has most given life significance in times previous to our own ends up at best a faint memory. It is yet rare today for the teaching of history to get a lot deeper than a chronicling of inventions, leaders, wars, and perhaps philosophical beliefs. The reason? The kind of approach to history I've suggested here—with events engaged at the level of meaning, and the evolution of meaning—requires us to draw on aspects of intelligence's complexity that we engaged deeply only in times past.

And the fact that much has been lost as well as gained in culture's story to this point also has more dramatically consequential implications. It makes the negative results if we fail to address the critical challenges that confront us in our time particularly stark and graphic. Just how it does provides important additional insight into Integrative Meta-perspective's mechanisms and also helps us further appreciate the importance of needed changes.

To fully get at these insights, we need some additional language. I've spoken as if formative process' finishing and polishing stage is followed immediately by more integrative mechanisms. But it helps to think of the two halves of formative process as separated by a further kind of dynamic. CST calls this in-between time simply Transition.

---

9 Such amnesias are not the only contributing factor with this loss. There is also the distancing between poles intrinsic to Creative Differentiation. But amnesias are necessary to what we witness and warrant special attention because of their implications.

People commonly refer to the kind of thinking that comes out of this Transitional period culturally as "postmodern."

Dynamics inherent to Transition are key to understanding both much that most stands out in current experience and why Integrative Meta-perspective has become so critically necessary. In first introducing Integrative Meta-perspective, I proposed that the fact that the changes that produce it involve more than just letting go of one stage and moving to another makes these changes unique in culture's story. Stepping over Cultural Maturity's threshold in fact calls into question the whole developmental orientation that has before defined growth and truth.

At Transition, these dynamics result in a critical quandary that at first might seem to be a show-stopper. CST calls it the Dilemma of Trajectory. Going further as we have no longer benefiting us. Indeed, it would seem almost to make no sense. I was making reference to this dynamic in Chapter One when I suggested that going further with thinking of wealth and progress as we have would leave us disconnected from aspects of ourselves essential to being human. In observing that today we confront a Crisis of Purpose, I was describing a kind of experience predicted by the Dilemma of Trajectory.

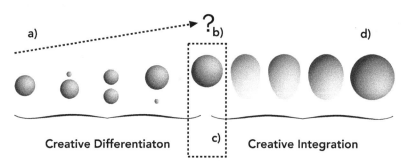

a) Cultural evolution's trajectory to this point

b) Transition (with more manifest sensibility at its peak and more germinal sensibilities largely eclipsed)

c) The Dilemma of Trajectory (with Cultural Maturity, or some similarly integrative process, needed to go on)

d) How Cultural Maturity reconciles the Dilemma of Trajectory

Fig. 3-4. The Dilemma of Trajectory

We can understand the Dilemma of Trajectory (see Figure 3-4) equally well in terms of intelligence's multiplicity or in terms of polarity. With regard to intelligence, the Dilemma of Trajectory leaves us even further distanced from ways of knowing other than the rational. With Transition, only the most surface levels of the emotional remain. And the more imaginal and body aspects of intelligence, if we are in touch with them at all, remain largely as sensibilities to be exploited for profit.[10]

To appreciate the implications when it comes to polarity, we can turn to how the relationship between archetypal qualities evolves over the course of any formative/creative process—and specifically how it has evolved over the course of history. History to this point has taken us from times in which the archetypally feminine played much the larger role (in tribal times, our connectedness with nature and the tribe defined truth and meaning) to times in which the archetypally masculine most often clearly prevails. Modern age belief acknowledges the archetypally feminine with the more romantic side of its heroic/romantic narrative, but more as decoration than substance. With Transition, the archetypally feminine becomes, in effect, eclipsed. We are left more and more distanced from aspects of our being to which the archetypally feminine has traditionally provided access. This "includes the receptive, the aesthetic, the experiential world of children, and any depth of connection with either our bodies or with nature. I sometimes joke that all we have left today from the ancient power of the receptive is shopping, social media, and eating—often to the point of obesity. I mean the observation only partly in jest.[11]

---

10 Some examples: Hands down, advertising is today's preeminent art form, at least if we measure preeminence in terms of dollars spent. And imaginal and body intelligence provide primary inroads for the addictive dynamics of video games. (See "The Arts" in "The Future of Cultural Domains" chapter in the *Cultural Maturity: A Guidebook for the Future* or the library section of the Cultural Maturity blog).

11 Notice that this picture at once affirms and fundamentally challenges contemporary critiques of "patriarchy." It affirms that we can't continue to go forward as we have. But because it also validates the importance of the process that has gotten us to where we are, it directly confronts beliefs that somehow make patriarchy in itself a problem. It also directly questions

The Dilemma of Trajectory's significance becomes even more stark and inescapable if we add the conceptual recognition that polarity at its most basic juxtaposes difference/distinction on one hand with unity/connectedness on the other. Each stage in formative process's first half is defined not just by greater distinction between poles, but also by a greater emphasis on difference more generally. At Transition, this defining impetus reaches an extreme. We are left in essence only with difference.

It is not surprising that the Dilemma of Trajectory might result in a felt Crisis of Purpose. It is hard to understand how continuing on in this direction could give us anything of value; indeed, how progressing in any way that might be consistent with life and meaning remains possible. And this apparent dead-end circumstance is amplified by an additional consequence of the Dilemma of Trajectory. The further distancing from intelligence's multiplicity that the Dilemma of Trajectory describes makes the kind of understanding needed to see anything that could take us forward essentially impossible. This is the case not just for the average person, but also for the people we tend most to look to for guidance.

I just noted how developmental amnesias can leave education unable to address more than the most surface layers of history. There is a more ultimately concerning consequence for education. In an earlier footnote, I proposed that higher education can today face inherent limitations when it comes to addressing the future. Academia's continuing tendency to make rational intelligence truth's last word and objectivist/materialist reality what it is all about[12] leaves it severely

---

advocacy that makes patriarchy only about male dominance. Over the course of history, women as well as men have come to embody more of the archetypally masculine and less of the archetypally feminine. In On the Evolution of Intimacy, I examine some of the implications of this more nuanced critique for current gender-related conversations.

12 The postmodern thread in academic thought in fact often challenges rationalist/objectivist/materialist thought quite directly. But the way that it does leaves it necessarily short of culturally mature understanding. Postmodern thought tends to make claims that CST would call "cross-polar." It is not unusual, for example, to find lengthy hyper-rational treatises on the limits of rationality.

limited when it comes to teaching needed new skills and capacities, and unable ultimately to deeply grasp a concept like Cultural Maturity. The simple fact that progress needs to be understood more systemically, in ways that take into account more than material measures, for example, can present a challenge to traditional academic thought. I've argued that if academia's historical assumptions about understanding are not challenged, they will increasingly get in the way of higher education providing leadership going forward.[13]

All these obstacles are real. And at the same time, the Dilemma of Trajectory's greatest significance may lie not with how it appears to give us nowhere to go, but with how squarely it places before us the inescapable necessity of the changes that Cultural Maturity makes possible. The Dilemma of Trajectory makes indelibly clear that if we restrict ourselves to what we have known, there is nothing we can do to rectify circumstances that will ultimately be our undoing. In another way, we recognize how Integrative Meta-perspective—or at least something that can produce change of a similarly integrative sort—becomes the only real option.

Transitional Absurdity

One further recognition is critical if we are to effectively understand today's particular circumstances. Again it requires some new language. What CST calls Transitional Absurdity provides explanation for much of what we can find most disturbing in current human behavior. It also helps us understand how what we see may have more benign—or at least more reconcilable—implications than we might fear.

It is hard to ignore that much that goes on in our times seems not at all sane. And we must not ignore it—we pay a high price when we do. At the same time, acknowledging how often our actions seem not sane easily leads only to a debilitating lack of hope. An observation that follows directly from what we have seen assists us in getting beyond both unhelpful responses: Many phenomena particular to our time that may appear ludicrous, if not disastrous, in their implications, are predicted by what CST describes.

---

13 See "Education" in "The Future of Cultural Domains" chapter in *Cultural Maturity: A Guidebook for the Future* or the library section of the Cultural Maturity blog.

Some of these phenomena are simple reactions to limits we would prefer to deny, or to complexities that stretch us beyond what we are yet able to tolerate. But many relate more directly to the Dilemma of Trajectory. I've described how Creative Transition's threshold presents a strange circumstance. The archetypally masculine has almost wholly eclipsed the archetypally feminine. We stand in a world of all content and no context, of all right hand and no left, of life as ultimate abstraction stretched ever more distant from the foundations of experience.

Applying the concept of Transitional Absurdity requires care. As with other tools of critique, it can become a repository for any phenomenon that our particular worldview might disagree with. We must understand it as a very specific concept requiring very particular discernments. But when we effectively grasp the concept, it provides essential insight and perspective.

Among the phenomena I consider Transitional Absurdities I include the extreme superficiality of mass consumer culture, how readily we ignore potentially catastrophic damage to the environment, and the partisan pettiness of so much of modern politics (which I've argued threatens to undermine the ultimate effectiveness of government). I also include the curious assumption that unfettered greed can produce stable economic systems that serve the larger good (for which there is no evidence) and how distanced we can be today from the body as experience (as we see with our modern infatuation with plastic surgery and our use of sex to sell most anything). I include, too, techno-utopian beliefs that assume that new technologies can solve all the world's problems. (I view techno-utopian thinking as a kind of postmodern fundamentalism.) We can understand each of these realities as what we would expect when a challenging of traditional assumptions intersects with developmental dynamics in which only the faintest vestiges of more archetypally feminine sensibility remain to ground our choices.

Perhaps surprisingly, the fact that we today see Transitional Absurdities is not all "bad news." These realities are inescapable and very real. And they are not just absurd; if we extend them any great distance into the future, they become insanity. But at the same time, the concept of Transitional Absurdity offers an ironic sort of reassurance.

We derive at least limited comfort from recognizing that such blindnesses and insanities are predicted. The creative necessity of Transition means that we need not think of Transitional Absurdity as evidence that we have gone irreparably astray. In addition, the same recognitions that make Transitional Absurdities predicted also support the conclusion that the potential for further, more mature changes are built into who we are. The concept of Cultural Maturity not only affirms the fact that solutions exist, it suggests that, in the end, a single solution—Integrative Meta-perspective and the cultural "growing up" that the concept of Cultural Maturity describes—works for all of these absurdities. We find both reason for optimism and needed guidance.

That Transitional Absurdities carried very far into the future become not just absurd, but insane raises some obvious questions about what we should anticipate in the decades immediately ahead. While Cultural Maturity points toward important new possibility, Transitional dynamics suggest something quite different if these absurdities continue on to any great degree. In fact, they most likely will. At any major culture change point we tend to hold onto old realities well beyond their timeliness. Overshooting the mark is pretty much how things work—partly out of fear and denial, partly because systems are not homogeneous. There will always be differences—and often great differences—in how far along individuals and populations are in their development.

The implications of this picture become more stark and immediate if we add the observation I made at the end of Chapter One regarding challenges that could be our undoing as a species. I described how successfully addressing concerns that could most easily be the end of us—such as nuclear annihilation, climate change and environmental destruction, partisan polarization with its capacity to undermine effective governance, old definitions of wealth and progress destabilizing economic systems and leaving us without an effective guiding narrative, or a failure to effectively manage emerging technologies—in each case requires new skills and capacities that become possible only with Cultural Maturity's cognitive reordering. The Dilemma of Trajectory and the concept of Transitional Absurdity also make a further reality more understandable that compounds the dangers that I pointed toward earlier. I suggested that experiencing one or more of these dystopian realities becomes essentially inevitable without Integrative Meta-perspective and the capacity for more mature choices that results. Continue on as we have and major calamity—and perhaps even the demise of the species—will be the inevitable result.

The Dilemma of Trajectory and the fact of Transitional Absurdities each provide both further support for how I have described the
workings of Integrative Meta-perspective and additional evidence for
Integrative Meta-perspective's necessity in our time. It is a harsh sort of
evidence. If this interpretation is not essentially correct, we are headed
in directions that are ultimately unworkable, with no options—at least
if we are limited to how we have thought in times past—that could
save us.

Where It Takes Us—Scenarios for the Future

One of the best ways to refine our understanding of Integrative Meta-perspective is to compare and contrast where its changes take us
with other outcomes. I divide the commonly encountered views of the
future into five "scenarios" (to use the language of futurists): We've Arrived scenarios, We've Gone Astray scenarios, Post-industrial/Informa-
tion Age scenarios, Postmodern/Constructivist scenarios, and Trans-
formational/New Paradigm scenarios. Each scenario can be understood
in terms of reflections from this and previous chapters. CST views
them less as logically arrived-at conclusions than as different ways that
now-outmoded patterns of cognitive organization leave us yet short of
Cultural Maturity's threshold.[14]

We've Arrived Scenarios

Many people today treat present social realities as a kind of cultural
end point—as most people through history have done with beliefs in
their times. Advocates of such "we've arrived" conclusions assume that
our current institutions and ways of thinking—whether political, religious, scientific, or economic—represent an apex, or at most need
a further bit of polishing. Integrative Meta-perspective directly challenges We've Arrived scenarios. While it affirms the achievements of
the Modern Age, it also makes clear that there is no more reason to
assume we've arrived at some culminating truth in our age than in any
age previous, and every reason to hope that we have not.

---

14 I address each of these scenarios in more depth in *Cultural Maturity: A
   Guidebook for the Future.* Extended articles in the Cultural Maturity blog
   (www.culturalmaturityblog.net) provide additional detail.

We've Gone Astray Scenarios

Certain other people today believe almost the opposite, that in some fundamental way humanity has failed, gone astray. We find extreme forms in millennialist religious warnings that the end is near, and milder versions in the more pessimistic of liberal/humanist and environmentalist positions (where legitimate concern can devolve into a self-fulfilling cynicism).

We've Gone Astray interpretations can include claims that are at least superficially consistent with culturally mature conclusions, such as that modern times often find us in denial about much that desperately needs our attention or that important truths—for example, about nature, about the sacred, about community, and more—have been "forgotten." But Integrative Meta-perspective just as fundamentally challenges We've Gone Astray scenarios. It argues that the future, at least in potential, holds great possibility. And it makes clear that going back to some perceived more ideal time is not the answer if we wish a healthy and vital future—not even if we wish to retrieve aspects of human understanding we perceive to be lost.

Post-industrial/Information Age Scenarios

I've made reference to this third kind of worldview in talking about the more heroic, archetypally masculine thread in modern understanding. Post-industrial/Information Age scenarios picture a future defined by continued "onward-and-upward" technological progress and assume that inventions yet to come hold the answers to humanity's problems.

Integrative Meta-perspective very much affirms the role of technological progress. And the best of Post-industrial/Information Age interpretations can sometimes get a toe over Cultural Maturity's threshold. For example, they may include the recognition that new technologies tend to bring with them new ways of thinking that have characteristics in common with culturally mature understanding. But Integrative Meta-perspective makes clear that inventing is not the same thing as using invention wisely. And it emphasizes that technological advancement alone can neither fully explain the changes we see today nor produce the changes we need for tomorrow.

More significantly, Integrative Meta-perspective confronts us with how a technological gospel, even if we include changes in thought that new invention may stimulate, not only stops short of a narrative able to provide reliable guidance or real inspiration, it presents real dangers. Of all the various versions of ideological belief I have touched on, it is techno-utopian beliefs that in the end have the greatest potential to result in truly cataclysmic consequences.

Postmodern/Constructivist Scenarios

I've made reference to postmodern belief with the CST concept of Transition. Postmodern thought has had major influence in recent decades, particularly in academia. It emphasizes today's loss of familiar cultural guideposts and final, "essentialist" truths in general. And it argues that we "construct" the realities we live in—and that the defining task of the future is to learn to do so more consciously.

Postmodern thinking at its best can at least bring us up to Cultural Maturity's threshold. For example, the observation that our human worldviews are "constructed" finds crude parallels in the conclusions of a creative frame. But postmodern thought in the end rarely succeeds in being culturally mature. Surrendering past cultural absolutes and choosing more consciously can only be a beginning. We must also learn to relate and think in new "post-essentialist"—more nuanced, dynamic, and systemic—ways.

Particularly with the more extreme of interpretations, postmodern thought commonly reduces to an ultimately unhelpful different-strokes-for-different-folks relativism. And its common aversion to overarching conception—indeed, conception of most any kind—means it leaves us with little of use to replace the traditional guideposts it so insightfully takes away. If we are not careful, postmodern belief can result only in aimlessness and cynicism. When such belief becomes ideology, it effectively undermines any ability to move forward.

Transformational/New Paradigm Scenarios

I've made reference to this strand in future-oriented thinking in talking about the more left-hand, romantic, archetypally feminine tradition in modern age understanding. Like Integrative Meta-perspective, Transformational/New Paradigm scenarios talk about changing cultural realities, but they frame these changes in the language of "changes in consciousness," or new spiritual and scientific "paradigms."

At their best, such beliefs again can at least approach Cultural Maturity's threshold. But most often they then fall decidedly short. Integrative Meta-perspective agrees that our times require that we think and perceive in new ways. But it also makes clear that the greater portion of Transformational/New Paradigm views, particularly of the more philosophically idealist or New Age sort, have more to do with wishful thinking than changes possible in our time. More pointedly, as often as not, such utopian pictures of change, even if they were possible to realize, imply realities and consequences that we would not want. (And the most simplistic of these views do not really describe anything new at all, but instead reflect idealized projections from the realities of times well past.[15])

Integrative Meta-Perspective

Integrative Meta-perspective's more encompassing vantage both helps us avoid traps that accompany each of these alternative interpretations of what may lie ahead and understand just why this array of interpretations is what we commonly see. It offers that we might step decidedly beyond the conclusions of each. It also lets us make sense of essential questions that none of these alternative narratives alone, or even together, can effectively frame, much less successfully answer.

---

15 Earlier I made reference to how people can confuse systems thinking with classical Eastern spiritual beliefs or with the beliefs of tribal societies.

CHAPTER FOUR

Applications and Implications— From Leadership and Love to a Needed New Maturity in Our Relationship with Death...and More

Applications and implications were where we started. In Chapter One, I described challenges that could well be the end of us without the more mature values and ways of thinking that come with Integrative Meta-perspective. The consequences of failing to successfully address the first four additional challenges I will touch on here—confronting the new realities today presented by leadership, love, gender, and the fact of our mortality—are not so obviously catastrophic. But effectively navigating the changes each presents will be essential to a vital human future. The last challenge I will touch on—device addiction when amplified by the dynamics of machine learning—is particularly provocative in how easily it could bring human advancement as a whole to a halt.

I've given special attention thus far to a small handful of themes that cut across needed new skills and capacities: getting beyond projection and polarization, acknowledging the fact of real limits, and learning to frame the truths we draw on (including our definitions of wealth and progress) in more encompassing—systemic—ways. I've also implied other themes, such as the importance of better acknowledging uncertainty and complexity, assuming new levels of responsibility, and learning to understand in ways that better take into account the fact of change. This chapter's additional examples further highlight all of these themes. They also provide an opportunity to introduce some further concepts and insights important to fully grasping Integrative Meta-perspective's implications and the more dynamic and systemic picture of reality's workings that results.

Rethinking Leadership

If I were asked for a single to word to describe what Integrative Meta-perspective is about, my answer would be "leadership." This includes both leadership in ourselves and leadership in the world. Integrative Meta-perspective is about assuming a new, more mature kind of authority and responsibility in everything that we think and do.

Most immediately, Integrative Meta-perspective results in a new kind of personal leadership, leadership in the workings of our psychological mechanisms. In leaving behind our historical reliance on culture as a mythic parent, we assume new responsibility for both the truths we draw on and for the consequences of our actions. And in more deeply engaging the whole of our tool-making, meaning-making complexity, we become capable of understanding in ways that are more nuanced and encompassing than we could have known before.

The fact that such more mature internal leadership involves greater uncertainty and requires new appreciation for complex interconnections and contingencies can at first feel unsettling. And the degree to which the outcome is in an essential sense quite common-sense and ordinary—how it involves only coming a bit closer to seeing things for what they are—can take us by surprise. But ultimately, such more "creative" internal leadership could not be more significant. It invites an essential new kind of power and sophistication in all of our personal choices.

Just as important, Integrative Meta-perspective alters how we understand formal leadership, of every sort—governmental leadership, business leadership, the leadership provided by teachers, doctors, religious figures, and more. In a similar way, in-the-world leadership in potential takes on a new kind of nuance, power, and sophistication.

Current circumstances help shine light on just what is changing and also why further changes are so important. Trust in leadership today is less than it was at the height of anti-authoritarian rhetoric in the 1960s. We could easily assume—and people have argued—that this modern lack of confidence in leadership reflects something gone terribly wrong—broad failure on the part of leaders, a loss of moral integrity on the part of those being led, or even an impending collapse of society.

Integrative Meta-perspective suggests an alternative interpretation. It follows from Cultural Maturity's cognitive reordering that our times should be requiring—and making possible—an essential "growing up" in how we understand, relate to, and embody leadership, wherever we find it. Such a new, more mature leadership picture makes major new demands, but Cultural Maturity's interpretation suggests a picture that is ultimately positive.

It helps to put today's new leadership realities in historical perspective. Formal leadership's evolution has involved not just what leadership looks like, but also what makes it leadership at all. Leadership as we customarily think of it arrived with our Modern Age—with the emergence of individual determination as a rallying cry and with the rise of democratic principles. New leadership assumptions and approaches then directly challenged the more heredity-based and dictatorial/authoritarian leadership practices of earlier times.

While these new steps represented important progress, a further chapter in how we conceive of and engage leadership will be essential for times ahead. The role of projection helps make sense of what more is needed. I've described how the chosen-people/evil-other social identifications of times past were based on projection. Mythologized projection has also always before been central to the workings of leadership. We've projected our power onto leaders.

Projective dynamics are most obvious with leadership of times well past. Leaders such as pharaohs and kings were seen, if not as gods, then certainly as god-like. But in a similar—if not quite so absolutist—way, we have continued to make leaders heroic symbols in modern times. I think of how John F. Kennedy was described using the imagery of Camelot and how explicitly Ronald Reagan assumed the role of a mythic father figure. We've symbolically elevated not just political leaders, but authorities of all sorts—religious leaders, professors, doctors, and leaders in business.

Projecting our power onto leaders, as with other projective dynamics, has served us. It has provided a sense of order in a world that would otherwise have been too complex and deeply uncertain to tolerate. But if how I have described Cultural Maturity's changes is correct, going forward will require more than leadership as we have known it.

Some further new language that follows from previous reflections on polarity and projection help get at what is most basic in the needed changes. With the leadership of times past, leaders and followers have functioned as opposite aspects of larger systemic dynamics. Leadership relationships have been what we could call "two-halves-make-a-whole" relationships. For leadership to serve us going forward, it must be of a more Whole-Person sort—or, given that it is happening collectively, we might better say of a more Whole-Person/Whole-System sort. The word "whole" as I use it here refers to the all-the-crayons-in-the-box kind of entirety that becomes possible with Integrative Meta-perspective.

Culturally mature leadership juxtaposes leaders and followers each able to embody their own all-the-crayons-in-the-box completeness. One result is that leadership becomes more powerful in its potential effects. Another result is that leadership becomes in important ways more ordinary and humble. Leaders become simply people respected for their ability and willingness to take on important and demanding jobs. Integrative Meta-perspective makes such Whole-Person/Whole-System leadership newly understandable and newly possible.

Do we currently see this kind of change in how we think about and embody leadership? Given today's crisis of confidence in leadership, the evidence might seem to suggest otherwise. But this diminishing confidence is also consistent with what we would predict as old forms of leadership give way to more culturally mature possibilities. It may be not so much that leaders are failing today, but that old forms of leadership are failing.

In fact, we see needed changes with authority relationships of many sorts, at least the beginnings of such changes. Some of today's most important Cultural Maturity–related advances link the opposite halves of authority-related polarities—teacher with student, doctor with patient, minister with churchgoer, president with populace. We are starting to see authority relationships of all sorts becoming more two-way, with more listening and flexibility on the part of leaders and more engaged and empowered roles for those who draw on a leader's expertise and guidance.

What we witness is not all positive. Leadership in our times provides an often all-too-graphic illustration of the awkward, in-between place that we so often reside in when it comes to Cultural Maturity's changes. We tend today to be much better at demanding the gift of more grown-up leadership than at knowing what to do with it. We may want leaders to get off their pedestals, but frequently when they attempt to do so, we respect them less, not more. And while we may wish that leaders were more transparent, that they would reveal more of themselves and make fewer decisions behind closed doors, often when they do, our first response is to attack them for their human frailties. Such awkward in-between responses can be frustrating, but they are consistent with the concept of Transition that I introduced in the previous chapter.

We also today often see regression of a troubling sort both in the actions of leaders and in the kind of leadership people can find attractive, as we've witnessed over the last decade with the rise of more authoritarian approaches to governmental leadership around the world. Whether this reflects simply the two-steps-forward/one-step-back nature of social change or a more deeply concerning kind of regression in the face of today's immense challenges is at this point hard to know. But whichever is the case, what we find is not wholly unexpected when set beside the various other Transitional Absurdities I've described.

Changes realized thus far in how we conceive of leadership can at best represent a place to start. But if the concept of Cultural Maturity is accurate, these beginnings presage a new kind of relationship to authority in all parts of our lives that should become ever more essential in times ahead.

The topic of leadership helps bring together the various themes that I've described as cutting across needed new skills and capacities. Most obviously, leadership's new picture is about stepping beyond assumptions based on projection and polarization. But in the end, it is just as much about limits, in this case about both limits to what leaders can provide and limits to what we can ultimately know. It is also about learning to ask more systemic questions and about drawing on more systemic and complete kinds of truth—including when it comes to wealth and progress. And each of the additional themes I've noted similarly plays a role, the importance of better tolerating uncertainty, of assuming new levels of responsibility, and of recognizing that everything must be understood in the context of time. Integrative Meta-perspective challenges us to engage a more explicitly creative picture of authority at all levels, from how we relate to ourselves, to the choices we make in our families and communities, to how we engage the planetary-level decisions on which our future will most depend.

The Myth of the Individual

These reflections on leadership provide a good place to introduce a pivotally important concept that I have only fully clarified in my own mind in recent years. I call it the Myth of the Individual. The Myth of the Individual alerts us to the possibility of thinking about identity in more complete ways. It also alerts us to the importance of doing so if the promise of real individual choice is to be realized.

It turns out that while we've tended to think of identity in modern times in terms of individuality, as yet we have not seen individuality in any full sense. In fact, as these reflections on the role that projection has played in leadership illustrate, our modern age concept of the individual stops short of what we have thought we were describing. I've observed that leadership in times past has been based on two-halves-make-a-whole relationships—relationships where each person represents half of a larger systemic entirety. Being half of a systemic whole is not yet about being an individual, certainly not in any fully realized sense. This distinction has major consequences for multiple parts of our lives—leadership being just one of them. That we might now recognize the Myth of the Individual follows directly from how Integrative Meta-perspective's more whole-box-of-crayons picture helps us more fully grasp what it ultimately means to be human.

Reflecting briefly on the last time in history we witnessed a fundamental shift in our thinking about identity helps bring the Myth of the Individual into finer focus. Our now familiar concept of the individual assumed its place on culture's stage with the more general emergence of modern age sensibilities. With the art of the Renaissance, for the first time, figures depicted were not just symbols, but mortals, and works of art were signed, marked as the achievements of particular people. Later, in the world of love, with the advent of the modern romantic ideal, we came to think of the bonds between men and women as now the province of individual inclinations. Over time, a more individualistic picture of identity transformed institutions of all sorts, giving us the Reformation's newly personal relationship to God, institutional democracy (with determination now a product of the votes of individuals), capitalist economic systems (based on competition between individuals), and modern higher education (increasingly a vehicle to prepare people for this degree of individual choice). These changes were hugely significant.

But there is no reason to assume that the modern age picture that resulted represents the end of the identity story. Modern age changes brought greater autonomy, certainly. But given that they were based on projection, they necessarily left us short of individual identity in any complete sense. With Integrative Meta-perspective, being an individual takes on a fundamentally different meaning. Individual identity becomes about consciously holding the whole of our multi-faceted complexity.

An additional way to think about the Myth of the Individual further ties it to Integrative Meta-perspective and has important implications for how we think about Whole-Person/Whole-System identity and relationship. It takes us back to the way I've spoken about polarity at its most basic, juxtaposing difference/distinction on one hand with unity/connectedness on the other. Our modern age concept of the individual identifies with difference—to be an individual is to be distinct. As such, it reflects only half of what it means to be an individual in a Whole-Person sense. Identity, when understood from Cultural Maturity's more whole-box-of-crayons vantage, is equally about difference and interconnectedness.

The Myth of the Individual is most obviously pertinent to how we think about personal identity and more dyadic leadership relationships—doctor with patient or teacher with student. But it also has provocative implications for the future of social institutions. Government makes a good example. We tend to think of modern representative government as a culminating ideal. Part of the argument for this conclusion is that modern institutional democracy is "government by the people." By this we mean government as an expression of individual choice. But while modern age democracy indeed involves greater choice than the governmental forms of any earlier cultural stage, if what I've described is accurate, democracy in the sense of whole people taking full responsibility for their choices is something we have not yet witnessed. This would require a further step in our evolution as choice-making beings.

We have not yet seen "government by the people" in the mature systemic sense that the concept of Cultural Maturity proposes is now becoming necessary. But if what I have described is accurate, such a next step becomes important to think about. It may very well be necessary to government that can work going forward.[1]

Rethinking Love

Our next topic—changes reshaping love in our time—brings the Myth of the Individual into particularly high relief and also helps us more fully appreciate what stepping beyond it requires of us. It also ties directly to these reflections on leadership—perhaps surprisingly, given that we often think of leadership and love almost as opposites. Integrative Meta-perspective invites us to take on a new, more complete and creative kind of authority in the experience we call love.

Thirty years ago, I wrote an article I titled "Beyond Romeo and Juliet: A New Meaning for Love." No piece I have written since has been more often cited. In it, I described how the phenomenon we call love is changing, and not just in the forms it takes, but also in terms of what makes it love at all. I proposed that we are being challenged to bring more to the experience of love than has ever before been necessary, and more than we human beings have before now been capable of.

For love's new picture to fully make sense, we need first to recognize that love does indeed change. Commonly we regard love to be timeless—we assume that love is love. But love has very much evolved over the course of history, with love as we tend to think of it—Romeo and Juliet–style romantic love—only one chapter. What we call love today is in fact a relatively recent cultural "invention"—a product of our modern age. People in the European Middle Ages often idealized romantic love, but it was unrequited love they put on a pedestal.

Even if we do recognize that love has changed through time, even changed in fundamental ways, we still tend to assume that love as we have known it most recently represents a kind of culmination. But this assumption, too, fails to hold up. If indeed love evolves, then there is no reason to believe that it should now stand still. And there is a deeper reason to question such last-word assumptions that parallels what I described

---

1   See *Cultural Maturity: A Guidebook for the Future* or the library section of the Cultural Maturity blog for more extensive reflections on leadership and the future of governance.

for leadership. It turns out that the modern age romantic ideal is not only not some final manifestation of love, in fact it represents something quite different from what we have assumed it to be about.

In another way, we confront the Myth of the Individual. We tend to think of—and idealize—modern romantic love as love based on individual choice. In the sense that romantic love has taken us beyond the historical practice of having partners chosen by families or matchmakers, it does indeed reflect greater freedom of choice. It also reflects an important step toward greater authority in our lives. But this is not yet individual authority in any complete sense—in the sense of choosing as whole people. The modern age romantic ideal again reflects two-halves-make-a-whole relating. Our task has been to find another person who would be our completion, our other half.

And there is more. Love as we have known it necessarily involves distortion. Similar to what we saw with us-versus-them thinking on the global stage and modern age leadership, with romantic love, we project parts of ourselves. I ascribe feminine aspects of myself to you; you ascribe masculine aspects of yourself to me. And as always happens with projection, we also mythologize the other, in this case making that person our answer and completion (or, at less pleasant moments, the great cause of our suffering). Not only is romantic love not yet love between separate people, it is not yet love that reflects who the two people involved actually are.

Because love of a two-halves-make-a-whole sort is all we have known, we can miss the fact that it has been incomplete in this sense. But the fact becomes obvious with reflection. Projection is what makes it possible for us to fall quickly in love with no real knowledge of the other person. It is also what makes it possible for the sound of wedding bells at a movie's conclusion to assure us that the protagonists will live "happily ever after" when, in fact, love's journey has barely begun.

The common result when we fall out of love provides even more inescapable evidence for this two-halves-make-a-whole mechanism. People tend to assume that we will then have distaste, even antipathy for the other person—which with high frequency proves to be what we in fact find. Notice that this outcome makes no sense if love had been between two whole people, if we have loved each other simply for who we are. The ending of such a relationship can bring sadness that something special has run its course. It can also bring regret that mistakes may have been made. But only in very unusual circumstances would antipathy be warranted. Why do we assume antipathy? When love involves projection, antipathy is needed in order to extract the projected part and regain our full sense of ourselves. The more common sentiment when love that is not based on projection fades is gratitude for what the other person has added to our lives.

Whole-Person love—love that draws on each person's whole-box-of-crayons complexity and sets aside the ready magnetisms of projection—represents a fundamentally different kind of connecting. With it, we better recognize how, as Lily Tomlin put it, "we are all in this alone." And simultaneously, we recognize the possibility of fuller ways of being together.

We may not at first celebrate love in this new sense. Leaving behind the romantic dream's promise that there is another person who can be our completion and answer may only look like loss. It is also the case that as yet we have little to guide us in engaging the changes this more mature kind of love requires of us. Imagery in the media, today, rarely gets much beyond the old romantic ideal—indeed, it rarely goes beyond absurd caricatures of it.

But when we begin to engage love as a Whole-Person dynamic, we quickly realize the power of what it offers. We see that that which has been taken away was ultimately illusion—an illusion that, while once necessary for love to work, today has become an obstacle. We also see how, because love of the more Whole-Person sort better reflects two people's unique lives, it can be much more significant—and thus more romantic in the deepest sense.

We encounter a further benefit of Whole-Person love in a version of the paradox I noted in first introducing Cultural Maturity's cognitive changes. There are important ways in which bringing greater maturity to love makes love simpler. Love becomes more about just being oneself and loving another person for who they are. It is about love simply as love. With this recognition, we can leave much of love's past trappings and expectations behind us if we so wish—we can shape love in the ways that best fit who we are together. It also becomes much easier to recognize and step beyond soap opera and drama that in the end only gets in the way of real relationship.

Whichever most stands out—the complexity or the simplicity—it is these changes that will allow love to remain something meaningful in the future. And with growing frequency, today, we find that we really don't have a choice. When one part of us tries to make someone else our solution, another part quickly acts to undermine it. We find ourselves creating struggle, doing something to put the other off, anything to regain our embryonic yet critical connection with a new sort of completeness in who we are. Increasingly it is possible to love only to the degree to which we can find ways to relate to another person while remaining fully ourselves.

The whole-box-of-crayons kind of connecting that gives us culturally mature love is not some luxury. The future of intimacy will depend increasingly on this ability to realize a fuller kind of relationship with ourselves and with those we care about. When today I work as a psychiatrist with couples, it is rare that the challenges and rewards of loving in new more mature and complete ways does not become a part of the conversation.

Gender and the Historical Battle of the Sexes

These reflections on the future of love are directly pertinent to a couple of topics that are today getting important new attention—how best to think about gender and right relationship between the sexes. I've mentioned that I regularly write articles about front-page-news issues where positions become polarized. When I attempted to do so with the #MeToo movement and related conversations about sexually violating behavior, I recognized that a simple article would not be sufficient. I saw that if I was to get at what was ultimately important, I would need to put relations between the sexes in historical perspective—indeed, very long-term historical perspective. I also saw that this would need to be the specific kind of historical perspective I referenced in the previous chapter in using intelligence's multiplicity and creative organization to map civilization's story. The eventual result was my most recent book, *On the Evolution of Intimacy: A Brief Exploration Into the Past, Present, and Future of Gender and Love*.[2]

---

2 Charles M. Johnston, MD, *On the Evolution of Intimacy: A Brief Exploration Into the Past, Present, and Future of Gender and Love*, 2019, ICD Press.

In taking on the story of gender, the book describes how the fact that historically we have tended to see men and women almost as op-posites is again a product of how traditional perceptions have been based on projection. Men have projected archetypally feminine aspects of themselves onto women, and women the reverse. In contrast, from Cultural Maturity's more whole-box-of-crayons systemic vantage, men and women come to seem much more similar than different.[3] The book also uses CST's mapping of how polarity has evolved over time to high-light how what it means to be a man or a woman has been predictably different at different times in history. It turns out that we need to look at the big picture and do so in a way that draws on the whole of intel-ligence's multifaceted complexity if we are to understand gender and relationship between men and women with needed depth and nuance.

I end the book by reflecting on the kind of effect contemporary gender conversations should have on the historical battle of the sexes. I propose that if such conversations can help us get beyond the projective dynamics of times past, they could result in important new levels of understanding. But I also suggest that the outcome, at least in the short term, could be almost the opposite. We could see a reactive/regressive response similar to that we find today with partisan pettiness in the political arena. What we eventually witness will depend on the degree to which conversations are informed by culturally mature sensibilities. Integrative Meta-perspective allows us to better see each other simply as people. In doing so, it opens the door to new, more mature levels of understanding and engagement.

To fully appreciate this conclusion and its implications, we need an observation that better puts what we see in the context of time. While

---

3 This is not to suggest some postmodern unisex ideal. CST uses the language of gender archetype as a way to get at both normative differences and the complexities of variation. The theory proposes that we see on average about a 60/40 balance of more archetypally masculine and archetypally feminine qualities consistent with gender. But it also delineates how, depending on a person's personality style, a man may embody more of the archetypally feminine than the average woman, and a woman may similarly embody more of the archetypally masculine than the average man. See *The Power of Diversity: An Introduction to the Creative Systems Personality Typology* or *The Evolution of Intimacy: A Brief Exploration Into the Past, Present, and Future of Gender and Love*.

the modern women's movement is important historically and to be applauded, I think of its contribution—with its goals of equal rights, equal opportunity, and equal safety—more as a culminating expression of the modern age project first begun with the Bill of Rights than as an aspect of the further kind of change this book is about. A simple way to see the difference is with how the kind of power implied by a phrase like "female empowerment" is almost entirely archetypally masculine power. Modern age belief defines power in "patriarchal" terms, whether the person identifies as a man or woman. A major contribution of culturally mature perspective is that it highlights the equal importance of archetypally feminine and archetypally masculine power.

We can recognize this important distinction in another way in how the modern women's movement tends to ascribe failings and needed learnings largely to men. I conclude *On the Evolution of Intimacy* with a chapter that lists "important lessons for men" and "important lessons for women." Integrative Meta-perspective challenges men and women equally, and does so in a manner that requires men and women each to engage fundamentally new ways of thinking and acting.

As with leadership, all the change themes I've touched on previously come into play with what love and gender today demand of us. Love and gender each require that we step beyond projection and mythologizing, that we accept limits to what we can be and what we can know, and that we draw on more complete kinds of truth—here, a more complete kind of relationship with both intimacy and identity. And, once more, greater comfort with uncertainty; a new, more ultimate kind of responsibility; and greater appreciation for the inescapability of change become necessary ingredients. With love and gender, we again make entry into a more dynamic and systemic—more ultimately "creative"—world of experience.

The Radical Implications of a New Maturity in Our Relationship with Death

I've proposed that a new, more mature relationship to limits represents one of Integrative Meta-perspective's most defining—and essential—results. We confronted the most obvious illustration in Chapter One with the inescapable fact of environmental limits. But I've at least implied other examples. Stepping beyond heroic models of leadership and romantic models of love each requires that we accept limits both to what one person can be for another and to what we can ultimately know.

I've given special attention through the years to one particularly ultimate kind of limit: death—the fact of our mortality. Because I am a physician as well as a futurist, the topic touches especially close to home. Here we will examine how any approach to health care delivery that can work going forward will require a new, more mature relationship with death. We will look too at how the way Integrative Metaperspective alters our relationship to death sheds valuable light on the future of other realms such as religion, science, and the media. It also provides important further evidence for Cultural Maturity's cognitive reordering and its significance.

Let's start with health care. The health care delivery debate in the end comes down to two concerns—access to care and cost containment.

The emotional vitriol that we've witnessed in recent years in attempting to deal with these issues has startled both politicians and the press. But, in fact, given what health care that is available and affordable will in the end require of us, it was totally predictable. The challenges that today's new realities present apply equally whatever a country's approach to health care delivery. In time, they will call into question even the most enlightened-seeming policies.

Health care expenditures are today spiraling uncontrollably—for everyone. Health care costs have increased at five times the rate of inflation over the last decade, with no natural end in sight. What we witness is ultimately no one's fault. Inefficiencies and excesses have played roles, but escalating costs have been primarily a product of modern medicine's great success. Early innovations—like sterile technique and penicillin—were relatively cheap. More recent advances—sophisticated diagnostic procedures, transplant surgeries, exotic new medications, and more—are increasingly expensive and promise only to get more so.

Escalating costs clearly can't continue indefinitely. They will eventually threaten not just medical care, but the health of economies. We face the fact that unless we wish to spend an ever-expanding percentage of national resources on health, we must in some way limit available medical services—or, if we wish to be more blunt and provocative in our language, in some way "ration" care. Initially this would involve restricting treatments of questionable efficacy—which we are already beginning to do. But eventually we would need to restrict care that could be effective, but that is simply beyond what we can afford.

Restricting care in this way puts before us a whole new order of ethical challenge. At the least, not providing care when we have effective care to offer calls into question modern medicine's defeat-disease-at-any-cost heroic mythology. But the challenge is deeper. Restricting care demands a new relationship to that most taboo of topics: the fact of death.

Medicine has always been about life-and-death decisions. But limiting care demands in effect the conscious choosing of death—at least in the sense of withholding care that might delay death's arrival. And this is the conscious choosing of death not for enemies or criminals, but for those we love, and ultimately for ourselves. Good long-term health care policy will require a maturity in our relationship with death that has not before been necessary, and, I would argue, in fact, has not before been possible.

I have met few people—and particularly in the political sphere—who recognize the full implications of the health care delivery crisis. Neither the more universal-care proposals put forward by the political left nor the more fee-for-service approaches advocated by the political right acknowledge, much less address, real limits. While ultimately untenable, such denial is understandable. Effectively addressing health care limits will in time make controversies around other death-related concerns such as abortion, assisted suicide, and capital punishment look like child's play.

Today we see beginning changes in how the health care world relates to death—only first steps, but steps of real significance. For example, we witness growing recognition of the importance of end-of-life conversations between patients and doctors. The role of quality hospice care is increasingly appreciated. And states are beginning to pass legislation that supports doctor-assisted suicide. Continuing to move beyond the Modern Age's heroic narrative when it comes to death will be more and more central to health care being a life-affirming enterprise in the decades and centuries ahead.

In writing about limits, I often emphasize how the rewards for acknowledging limits of an inviolable sort include not just avoiding the unpleasant consequences of denial, but also the recognition of options not otherwise visible. This is very much the case with health care limits. Confronting them more directly should contribute to increasingly mature and empowering insights regarding not just access to care, but also what it takes to be healthy, what it means to heal, and, more broadly, about the requirements of a healthy society. Start addressing such limits and pretty soon we begin examining questions that expand the health care picture dramatically. For example, we might ask, "Wouldn't it make sense to spend more of our resources on prevention?" And then, "If prenatal care is valuable prevention, what about good nutrition?" And we could go on. "If good nutrition is important, what about the effects of poverty, and lack of housing, ... and today's larger Crisis of Purpose." For today, isn't that just what the doctor ordered—a fresh, really big-picture look at the whole health care endeavor?

Medicine is not the only sphere where a "growing up" in our human relationship with death would have a fundamentally transforming effect. For example, it could bring important new perspective to religion. Appreciating how this might be the case further highlights the fundamental newness—and radical significance—of today's needed new, more mature relationship with death.

We could easily think that religion is a sphere that long ago made its peace with death. Funerals most commonly take place in churches, and religious settings are where we are most likely to encounter conversations about our mortality and find solace in the face of death. And if we go back to early cultural times, we often find death-related imagery closely tied to spiritual experience, as with how burial mounds were places of worship for the ancient Celts, and how writings such as the Tibetan Book of the Dead and the Egyptian Book of the Dead have served as guides to spiritual realization. But religion, by providing unquestioned explanation for what happens after death, has also served to protect us from death as experience.

To fully appreciate the challenge a culturally mature relationship with death presents to traditional religious teachings, it helps to step back and look at how religion has conceived of death through history. Each stage in the evolution of spiritual/religious understanding has provided us with a somewhat different picture of what happens after we die. In tribal times, death was thought of as bringing a rejoining with nature and also a reconnecting with our ancestors in a kind of parallel world. Later, with the early rise of civilizations and more polytheistic sensibilities, we commonly encounter belief in reincarnation, with death bringing a return to the present in some new form. With the emergence of monotheism, we came to think of death as providing entry into a now separate world—depending on our life choices, of either a heavenly or hellish sort. With the more liberal monotheism of modern age times, we tend most often to think of that separate world as simply a better and happier place. In a way consistent with its defining cultural stage, each of these explanations offered solace and gave us a way to reconcile with death. But each also, in the end, protected us from the fact of death. Each let us keep the easily overwhelming implications of facing death directly at a safe arm's length.

What about religion in the future? We confront some fascinating new questions when we combine the fact that Integrative Meta-perspective results in a new maturity in our relationship with death with religion's traditionally close association with end-of-life concerns. For example, if religion were to succeed in making the kind of transformational step I have argued will be necessary for medicine, might religion then come to better serve us at the end of life? And in the process, are there fundamental ways in which religious teachings might become different?

In asking such questions of religion, it is only fair to inquire in similar ways of science. A person could assume that Integrative Meta-perspective would make science's alternative conclusion—that death is just death, the end of us—instead correct. But science's explanation is ultimately just as much an "article of faith." Scientists share with theologians the fact that neither can describe death from personal experience. And Integrative Meta-perspective takes death's challenge to science an important step further. I've described how the kind of "objectivity" that science relies on, while a powerful tool, remains incomplete. The particular aspects of intelligence that the traditional scientific worldview leaves out—those most closely tied to the more germinal and mysterious aspects of experience—means that we should expect scientific interpretation to be especially unhelpful when it comes to making sense of death. In the end, science faces its own versions of the same questions that I suggested for religion, and the implications of addressing them could be just as transformative.

Integrative Meta-perspective supports death's challenge to the thinking of both religion and science in a further, more abstract way. I've described how any time we encounter beliefs that we think of as opposites—as we tend to do with religion and science—something important is likely missing in each kind of belief. We've seen how a more systemic picture will not only bring each kind of traditional conclusion into question, it will highlight how all along we've been keeping the hard and necessary question at arm's length. Might we not appropriately expect this to be the case with death?

A greater maturity in our relationship to death could also have marked and surprising effects in cultural domains that themselves do not as directly engage questions of death's significance. Here I think most immediately of the media, both serious media—such as news media—and media of a more entertainment sort. With regard to news media, news of an "if it bleeds, it leads" sort commonly garners the greater portion of airtime. And with media of the more entertainment sort, it is rare to find television after nine o'clock in the evening that doesn't involve at least one killing (and usually more). And killing—and the possibility of being killed—is pretty much what "action" movies and most popular video games are about.

Modern media commonly draws us in by creating a narrative tension between life and death. But, in the end, this is a manufactured tension, or at least a tension born of an increasingly outmoded and unhelpful interpretation of death—a polarized and mythologized picture that makes death, if not evil, certainly our adversary. I find it fascinating to reflect on how the kind of "growing up" in how we view death that the concept of Cultural Maturity describes might, in the long term, alter media—of all sorts.

The need for a new maturity in our human relationship with death also has a more overarching kind of pertinence in how directly it ties to today's Crisis of Purpose. I've argued that we find its necessary antidote in asking about what matters in deeper and more complete ways. Coming face to face with mortality in our individual lives teaches us about what most matters to us as individuals—death is a personal life's most pointed teacher of meaning, and ultimately of wisdom. As we learn to engage death collectively with a new maturity, it is reasonable to think that this engagement should help us in a similar way to more deeply confront what most ultimately matters to us more broadly—as humans.

Death confronts us with the fact that life as we know it ends. But it also confronts us with what is an even more final and easily disturbing limit. Death confronts us with limits to what is possible to control, and perhaps ultimately to understand. The humility required to accept this limit should play an essential role in helping us generate the wisdom that effective future decision-making in all parts of our personal and collective lives will increasingly require.

With the topic of death, we again recognize all of Integrative Meta-perspective's themes, not just limits. We confront the need to "bridge" polarities—between political advocacies with health care, with religion and science, and also more philosophically in how we conceive of the relationship between life and death. As I've just suggested, in a quite ultimate sense we also confront the importance of addressing what matters to us more systemically. And once again, we also encounter the importance of better acknowledging uncertainty (which death in the end makes inescapable), accepting a more final kind of responsibility (in our lives as a whole), and being more cognizant of the role that change plays in our experience of meaning (both with how our relationship with death has changed through history and with death itself as an ultimate expression of change). In another critical way, Integrative Meta-perspective challenges us to engage a more dynamic and systemic—more ultimately "creative"—picture of life's workings.

Device Addiction and Machine Learning— a Mix That Could Well Be the End of Us

I'll conclude this chapter with a couple of topics—device addiction and machine learning—that come together in a decidedly troubling way. The aspect of today's broader addiction epidemic that I find of greatest concern for the long term is not addicting drugs or obesity, but addiction to our electronic devices. And the dangers that device addiction present are amplified dramatically when we add the mechanisms of machine learning. Because the result could so easily sneak up on us and defies ready solutions, it can be legitimately argued that of all the dangers that I have addressed, it is this that could most easily be our undoing.

Cultural Maturity's cognitive changes are directly pertinent. We will see how today's Crisis of Purpose both increases the risks and provides insight into what will be needed to escape calamity. And we will examine a further kind of insight that requires Integrative Meta-perspective and that will be key if we are to avoid this result—understanding the fundamental differences between human intelligence and "artificial intelligence."[4] Each of these recognitions relates to an additional new-capacity theme beyond those I have previously emphasized—the broader task of effectively managing emerging technologies.

First, device addiction. While our electronic devices can do so many things that we find useful—and are often just plain fun—if we are to use them wisely, we need to examine not just what they can do, but our relationship to them. With growing frequency today that relationship is not a healthy one. Numerous writers have described concerns, for example, with how screen time can get in the way of developing real relationship skills and result in increased rates of depression. But the greatest danger is more basic. Too often our devices addictively hijack our attention—and our lives.

To grasp how this might be so, it helps to better understand the mechanisms of addiction. Addiction works by providing artificial substitutes for real fulfillment. In an experiment often described in psychology classes to teach about addiction, wires are run from excitement centers in a rat's brain to a depressible pedal in its cage. After the rat discovers the pedal, it pushes it with ever greater frequency, in the end abandoning other activities including eating, and dies.

Device-related addictive mechanisms are most obvious with video games, where shootings and explosions create readily repeatable jolts of excitement. But addictive dynamics present arguably even greater dangers with more everyday electronic devices such as cell phones—in part just because cell phones and the like have become aspects of most everyone's lives, in part because of the immense commercial rewards that come with their ability to manipulate our choices.

Several times a week I walk around a lake near my home in Seattle. (It is in one of the city's most popular parks.) Over a third of the people walking around the lake do so while staring at their cell phones. Often this is the case even for couples. Not only are they missing the beauty

---

4 You will note that I will rarely use the phrase "artificial intelligence," choosing instead to speak of "machine learning." This critical difference is the reason.

of the lake, they are substituting the stimulation of their devices for real relationship, a phenomenon we see with growing frequency more generally with social media. I've found myself seriously wondering if this is what science fiction writers have been anticipating with images of a zombie apocalypse.

People's attachment to their devices is not simply a product of the device's usefulness. It is a dirty little secret of the tech world (fortunately becoming less of a secret) that programmers consciously design their software to be addictive. They build in dynamics that make visiting a favorite site like playing a slot machine. The result is biochemical responses that have us feel anxiety if we are away from our devices for long. The fact that most of the content on our cell phones is advertising-driven means that we should find addictive mechanisms becoming only more sophisticated in times ahead.

Device addiction takes on particular significance with Transitional changes and today's Crisis of Purpose. As a start, these phenomena make us more vulnerable to addiction. As traditional cultural beliefs stop providing needed guidance and social connections, artificial substitutes for significance become increasingly attractive. And the Dilemma of Trajectory and the common intrusion of Transitional Absurdities can leave us feeling even further distanced from anything that matters.

Transitional dynamics also mean that we pay a particularly high price—and not just personally, but as a species—when we confuse addictive pseudo-significance with meaning. I've described how the antidote to our modern Crisis of Purpose lies ultimately in a fresh engagement with culture's Question of Referent.[5] We need to be asking what most matters to us collectively with new depth and courage. Being distracted and addicted makes success with this critical task essentially impossible. In this context, the selling of addictive substitutes for meaning could not pose a greater risk or be more ultimately immoral—in the sense of diminishing who we are and undermining future possibility.

As yet, few people sufficiently recognize either the depths of the dangers that device addiction presents or how impervious device addiction can be to solutions. I often work in therapy with young people. It is rare

---

5 See Chapter One.

that they don't come in addicted to their electronic devices. Young men tend most often to be addicted to video games. With young women it is more often the pseudo-relationship of social media that provides the hook. Addressing addiction to electronic devices can be particularly difficult. I often comment that I find addiction to opioids easier to treat.

The risks that accompany device addiction are amplified dramatically—indeed exponentially—when we add the mechanisms of machine learning. A defining characteristic of machine learning algorithms is that if a person gives them a goal, they will pursue that goal unquestioningly and unceasingly. Assign to such an algorithm the task of maximizing traffic to a website, for example, and it will do so irrespective of what it may take to accomplish this end. This fact has an easily missed but deadly consequence. Because addictive dynamics provide the most reliable way to get such attention, there is no need to design digital systems to be addictive. Over time, the inevitable result is ever more powerful digital designer drugs.[6] Dangers are further amplified by the fact that human operators commonly don't have access to the underlying machine learning processes (and commonly could not understand them if they did—the processes are just too multifaceted).

I think of three scenarios in which machine learning could have truly cataclysmic consequences. In the first, some kind of bad actor on the world stage wages an AI-based attack on a perceived enemy. The goal could be the destruction of physical infrastructure such as electrical grids and water supplies, disruption of communications networks, or, as we have seen attempted in very rudimentary form with Russian interference in elections, a fundamental undermining of social and governmental structures. We legitimately include this kind of application when we think of "weapons of mass destruction." In time, it may prove the most problematical example of such weaponry.

The second scenario is what people in the technology world most often point toward when they warn that AI could have cataclysmic results. Systems applying machine learning could eventually outcompete us. It is easy to make the goal of a machine learning algorithm simply to have the

---

6 Another inevitable result is "fake news." It turns out that the polarized emotionality of fake news makes it more effective for getting attention than the real thing.

mechanism propagate itself. Since such algorithms can be single-mind-ed in their competitiveness in ways that we humans will never be, and would never want to be,[7] the likelihood is high that they would prevail.

But I think the greatest danger lies ultimately with addictive dy-namics and the way machine learning could make those dynamics so overwhelmingly powerful that we would have no real defense. Put in systems terms, the result could be a runaway feedback loop that we have no way to understand, much less control. As the consumption of artificial stimulation increasingly replaced meaningful activity in our lives, we would become less and less able to discern the choices that would most ultimately benefit us. This is a scary picture, and not just a possible picture. Increasingly we see its beginnings in our daily lives. A good argument can be made that it is inevitable.

Is there anything we can do to counter this great potential danger? An approach I use with any addiction, but also in particular with de-vice addition, helps point toward what ultimately will be necessary. It turns addiction's own mechanisms—the substitution of artificial fulfill-ment for the real thing—against it.

I've mentioned that I often work with young people where device addiction is a concern. I will commonly start by asking the person ques-tions about what they most like to do, simple questions that help re-veal what uniquely matters to the person. We talk together about the importance of honoring and protecting the things that for them most create meaning. I then confront the person with how the addiction, in providing an artificial substitute for fulfillment, is undermining and doing damage to real fulfillment. I help the person practice living their life in ways that say yes to the real thing and no to the imposters. The therapy process becomes an exercise in making life-affirming choices. I've described how addressing addiction to electronic devices can be particularly difficult. But with persistence and commitment, this gen-eral approach will tend to be successful.[8]

---

7   In spite of how we often frame human nature in simplistic Darwinian fight-for-survival competitive terms, humans—thankfully—are more complex than just this.

8   Research on addiction provides provocative support for the power of signif-icance as an antidote. Addiction studies with rats have traditionally been

Related intervention at a broader cultural level immediately confronts obstacles. It will require not just that people appreciate the extent of the danger, but also that they are sufficiently connected to what matters in their lives that they can effectively discern when a particular activity serves them and when it does not. As I've suggested, this is a depth of connection that is too often lacking with Transitional dynamics and our modern Crisis of Purpose. But the basic principles of what needs to happen are very similar. And Cultural Maturity's changes make it possible for us to do what we need to do.

One particular recognition needs to be central if we are to avoid the kind of runaway mechanisms that could result in the combination of addictive dynamics and machine learning being the end of us. It brings us back to reflections in the previous chapter on the nature of intelligence. We need to better appreciate just how machine learning and human intelligence are different. In fact, machine learning and human intelligence work in ways that are hardly related at all, an observation that for someone like myself who works every day with intelligence's multilayered complexities is so obvious it hardly needs stating.

One difference is particularly pertinent to the dynamics of addiction and where needed solutions lie. I've described how machine learning is single-minded in pursuing its goal. There is an important sense in which human intelligence is not just more complex in all it considers, it is by its nature purposeful. This recognition is somehow always central in my work as a therapist. There is no need for me to work specifically to help a person live a more meaningful life. Indeed, if I believe this is my task, I risk undermining the desired outcome (it is too easy to end up imposing one's own notions of purpose). Instead, as I just described with the example of addressing addiction, all I need do is ask the person in different ways what most matters to them. Challenge the person to shape their life in ways that honor their answers, and purposeful choices will be the result. Put in CST terms, human

---

done with the animals in small, restrictive cages. In work done by Bruce K. Alexander, author of *The Globalization of Addiction, A study in Poverty of the Spirit*, rats that were put in highly enriched environments with toys and other rats to play with were shown to be much less vulnerable to becoming addicted to opioids.

intelligence is inherently creative. It seeks out the solutions that are most affirming of life. More than this, it seeks out the options that will be most consistent with generativity, with the possibility of newly vital expressions of life.

Another way to describe this same conclusion has particular relevance to the challenges presented by device addiction. There is an important sense in which human intelligence is ultimately moral. This claim may seem radical given how frequently we are not at all moral in our everyday dealings. And given how often history confronts us with acts for which we should not at all be proud, the claim might seem preposterous. But most often in our daily lives we act with basic kindness. And history's big picture finds humanity bringing ever greater complexity to its moral discernments.

This last observation has pertinence for these reflections both because it further highlights the inherently purposeful/moral nature of human intelligence and because it invites the intriguing question of whether new moral capacities might become possible in the future. In earliest societies, much that we would today consider totally unacceptable was common—for example, human sacrifice, slavery, and even cannibalism. The rise of civilizations saw more formal attention given to philosophical questions, but as we witnessed with the early Greeks and Egyptians, at least slavery continued as a common practice. The appearance of monotheism brought with it greater emphasis on moral concerns, but the resulting moral absolutism often left us still far from what we would find acceptable in our time. The Middle Ages gave us the Magna Carta, but it also brought the barbarism of the Crusades and the Spanish Inquisition, with thousands of people executed simply for their beliefs. In our Modern Age, we've witnessed important additional steps, with, for example, the Bill of Rights and its stated freedoms not just for religion but for speech more generally. And with the last century, we've seen essential further advances—for example, with the civil rights and women's movements, and more recently with advocacy for the rights of people with differing sexual orientations.

None of this is to suggest that we are always moral in our actions. Commonly we are far from it. My point is simply that there is clearly something in what it means to be human that is allied not just with advantage, but with a larger good. And it is embedded deeply enough that we can think of the human narrative as a whole as a story of evolving moral capacity. Human intelligence by its nature engages us in questions of value and purpose. We are imperfect beings, but we are also in the end moral beings. In contrast, machine learning is a tool, and while it is one with great potential for good, there is nothing in it that makes it inherently good, and much that makes it vulnerable to being a force for the opposite.

We need to address a question embedded in this distinction if we are to use machine learning in ways that ultimately serve us: Just what is it that makes human intelligence purposeful, and moral? The previous chapter's reflections provide the needed insights. CST proposes that the key lies in human intelligence's multiplicity. Human intelligence, with its multiple aspects, is not just more complex than can be modeled with a computer, it reflects a wholly different *kind* of complexity. I've described how the way human intelligence is structured makes it inherently "creative." By virtue of our multiple intelligences, we are not just inventive, but also inherently purposeful—and moral—in our actions.

For the sake of simplicity, we can think of the mechanisms of machine learning as roughly parallel to those of one specific aspect of human intelligence—the rational. In fact, machine learning, even at its best, mimics rational processing only imprecisely. If we look closely at rationality, we see that it functions in ways that are more subtle and layered than we tend to assume. But the analogy works adequately as a point of departure for grasping the basic strengths and limitations of machine learning.

The idea that we might have machines that can carry out many of the more rational/mechanistic tasks of cognition—and much more rapidly and complexly than we can—is a great thing. But as I've made clear with previous reflections on intelligence's multiplicity, rationality alone is not sufficient if we are to effectively engage the future's important challenges. Certain purely technical challenges can be addressed in this way, but not concerns that in any way include values, human relationships, or creativity of any deep sort—as most any questions that really matter to us eventually do. The common belief that machine learning could eventually address all of our concerns is not based on evidence. Rather, it is a product of the defining role that rational intelligence has played in modern age understanding. Extended into the future, such belief becomes a particularly dangerous expression of Transitional Absurdity.

These reflections on how machine learning and human intelligence are different have both good-news and bad-news implications.
On the good-news side, they mean that the more complex and sophisticated kind of thinking needed to make the required discernments is
not only possible, as potential it is built into who we are. Integrative
Meta-perspective again provides a solution. On the bad-news side,
they mean that appreciating what is needed if we are to make good
choices becomes very difficult without at least the beginnings of culturally mature skills and capacities. Today we so readily idealize the
technological (with Transition, we can, in effect, make it our god)
that we can get things turned around completely. Caught in techno-
utopian bliss, we can make machine learning what we celebrate. And
when we add addictive dynamics, the needed way forward becomes
ever more difficult to recognize.

Effectively managing machine learning and its effects will require
drawing on the purposeful/moral nature of human intelligence and doing so with whole new levels of sophistication. Every step of the way,
we have to ask whether particular applications benefit us in the sense of
being ultimately life-affirming. We also have to be exquisitely sensitive
to possible unintended consequences. (It is unintended consequences,
rather than malevolence, that are most likely to be our undoing.) Moving forward effectively will require not just applying a moral lens, but
bringing to bear an encompassing maturity of moral decision-making
that before now would have been beyond us to grasp.

I've noted that this section's reflections bring attention to a further
new-capacity theme. Integrative Meta-perspective helps us better assess risk. It helps us better assess technical risks. It also helps us better recognize risks that follow from how we think. With Integrative
Meta-perspective, we become better able to appreciate that our tools,
however amazing they may be, are only tools. This acknowledgment is
key if we are to use our tools in ways that will ultimately serve us. It is a
fact that becomes obvious—common sense—with Cultural Maturity's
cognitive changes. With Integrative Meta-perspective, we no longer
confuse ourselves with our tools. And certainly we stop mythologizing
our tools, treating them as gods.

While the power of machine learning to amplify additive dynamics
represents only one example of how such mythologizing can put us at

risk, it puts potential consequences in particularly high relief. If you came upon a person who, being especially fond of his hammer, put it on an altar and burned incense in its honor, you might find him weird, but let it pass. If, however, the hammer the person worshipped was capable of rising up on its own, hitting the person on the head and killing him—and perhaps killing everyone else in the process—then you would appropriately consider the person insane. That is the reality that we face today with machine learning. It can serve us richly as we go forward. But it can do so only if we are clear in our understanding of what it is and what it is not.

The challenges presented by device addiction, particularly when its mechanisms are digitally amplified, again bring each of the three main themes I've emphasized into play. Most immediately important is that reflected in our third theme, the need to revisit culture's Question of Referent and think about what most matters to us in more encompassing ways. I've described how today's Crisis of Purpose at once makes us vulnerable to addiction and provides insight into needed solutions. The antidote to the pseudo-significance that makes addiction attractive lies ultimately in engaging the more complete understanding of significance that Integrative Meta-perspective begins to make possible.

But we also recognize each of the other themes I've noted. We see the need to get beyond polarized thinking in how effective risk assessment requires that we leave behind both techno-utopian beliefs and their dystopian counterparts. We again confront the need to acknowledge real limits, in this case limits both to what we can do and to what we can understand and control. And engaging either intelligence's multiplicity or today's Crisis of Purpose requires that we better accept the fact of uncertainty, assume a more ultimate kind of responsibility, and become more comfortable with change's role in the experience of meaning.

Here we've added to our previous themes how Integrative Meta-perspective offers that we tool-makers might learn to use our tools in ways that are not just clever, but ultimately wise.

CHAPTER FIVE

Tools for Getting There—
The Provocative Power of Parts Work

I've approached introducing the concept of Cultural Maturity over the years in multiple ways. In my books *The Creative Imperative* and *Pattern and Reality*, I came at the task developmentally, by examining the creative parallels between different sorts of formative dynamics and what these parallels suggest about our particular time in culture as a creative process. In *Necessary Wisdom, Hope and the Future*, and *Cultural Maturity: A Guidebook for the Future*, I focused on the new skills and capacities needed to address today's critical challenges. And with my book *On the Evolution of Intimacy*, I turned to one issue where really big-picture, developmental perspective is needed—the history, present, and future of gender and love. With this volume, I've drawn a bit on each of these approaches, but my primary tack has been different yet. We've looked as directly as possible at the cognitive mechanisms that give us Integrative Meta-perspective's whole-box-of-crayons kind of systemic understanding.

Each of these ways of coming at where Cultural Maturity's changes take us can be used to facilitate Integrative Meta-perspective. Grasp any of them deeply and the result will be at least beginning steps into culturally mature territory. But we can also facilitate Integrative Meta-perspective more directly. Creative Systems Theory includes approaches specifically designed for this task.

The most significant approach I call simply Parts Work. A person must be developmentally ready for Parts Work for it to be effective. But if this is the case and Parts Work is done well, the approach leaves almost no option but to embrace experience from a more systemic vantage. In psychotherapy, where the work focuses at a personal level, this may be the more limited systemic vantage needed to address a particular conflicted issue or perhaps the somewhat more encompassing systemic vantage that accompanies personal maturity. But the approach can also be extended to bring about the more fully inclusive kind of systemic perspective that defines Cultural Maturity. Parts Work then becomes a tool for practicing culturally mature leadership and understanding, both within oneself and in one's engagement with the outer world. Here we take a look.

Parts Work

With Parts Work, a person engages the various aspects of him- or herself—the different crayons in that person's internal systemic box— as if they were characters in a play. Because of the way this is done, the person learns both to take more conscious authority in his or her life and to draw more deeply on the diverse sensibilities that make that person uniquely who he or she is. When the work happens at a more cultural level, Parts Work engages the person in drawing consciously and deeply on the diverse sensibilities and inclinations that make us who we are as humans.

A brief introduction: Parts Work starts with the person choosing a question or concern he or she wishes to explore. In asking the question, the person sits in what will eventually be his or her Whole-Person perspective (personally mature—or perhaps, eventually, culturally mature perspective) chair. The person is then guided in placing various parts— perhaps a curious part, an angry part, a reasonable part, an intellectual part, a sexual part—around the room. Each part is given its own chair. Through first stating the question and then engaging in conversation about it with the various parts, the person learns to draw on and apply his or her larger—whole-box-of-crayons—complexity. One result is the possibility of more useful answers to one's question. Another is practice in holding experience more systemically. Through the dual process of simultaneously exercising authority from the Whole-Person chair and drawing deeply on the diverse viewpoints that parts represent, the person becomes increasingly facile at engaging experience in more conscious and complete ways.

Three related cardinal rules guide the Parts Work process. Each ties directly to how our cognitive mechanisms become different with

Integrative Meta-perspective. First, only the Whole-Person chair interacts with the world. This guarantees that interactions will be of a Whole-Person/Whole-System sort. Second, parts don't talk to the world, only to the Whole-Person chair. This contrasts with what we see with reactive personal responses and more absolutist social assertions, where parts commonly do the talking. And third, parts don't talk with other parts. Shortly we will look at how polarized beliefs, both of a personal sort and those found with shared cultural belief systems, can be thought of as having their roots in talk between parts.

Parts Work provides a further useful shorthand image for the changes that produce Integrative Meta-perspective to add to Cultural Maturity's threshold (with the "bridging" of polarities) and our now familiar box of crayons. We can think of Cultural Maturity's cognitive reordering as a kind of "rewiring." It's an approach that requires some explanation, but it succeeds in getting beyond the Dilemma of Representation and adds valuable conceptual nuance. The images in Figure 5-1 depict "wiring diagrams" before and after doing Parts Work.

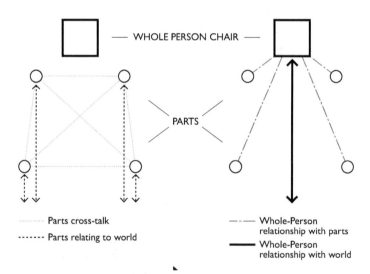

Fig. 5-1. Parts Work and Cultural Maturity's Cognitive Rewiring

The three cardinal rules help clarify what becomes different. Before doing the work, "wires" go from parts to the world. Afterward, we find only connections from the Whole-Person chair. In a similar way, before doing Parts Work, "wires" go back and forth between parts. Afterward, "wires" between parts, like those between parts and the world, are cut. Internal connections go only between parts and the Whole-Person identity chair.

As a therapist and also someone interested in change of a broader cultural sort, over the years I've come to draw more and more on Parts Work as an approach. I don't know of other techniques that apply all of intelligence's multiple aspects so simply and unobtrusively. I also don't know of other ways of working that so directly support culturally mature understanding, not just through what is said, but through every aspect of the approach, even the layout of the room. The three cardinal rules mean that Parts Work directly supports identity of the more complete sort I described with the previous chapter's look at the Myth of the Individual. And all that the Whole-Person chair draws on means that the understanding that results will be of culturally mature leadership's at once more powerful and more humble sort. Of particular importance at the level of process, the fact that I as a therapist speak only to the Whole-Person chair (in keeping with the first cardinal rule) means that my relationship with the client directly models and affirms relationship of a more Whole-Person sort.

Parts Work is not a "quick fix," even if the focus is primarily on concerns of a more personal sort. But engaged over time, more complete ways of thinking and acting follow naturally from the process. And if the person wishes to take on more cultural-level questions, Cultural Maturity's more encompassing changes will more and more come to seem obvious and straightforward. Even if a person does not specifically practice the various new skills and capacities that I've addressed in previous chapters of this book, he or she will find them seeming increasingly like common sense.

Along with being a powerful change tool, the Parts Work process, especially when done with cultural-level concerns, offers important conceptual insights. For example, it provides confirmation for my claim early in the book that ideological beliefs are "single-crayon" beliefs, that they reflect identification with systemic aspects. In doing Parts Work, people find it increasingly obvious that parts by their nature hold simplistic and limited beliefs. People also see that allowing parts to talk to the world (in violation of the second cardinal rule) results in reactive and ideological assertions.

This relationship between parts and ideology becomes particularly graphic when a person addresses questions that involve polarized advocacy. That can be around a particular issue or around competing cultural belief systems, as we can see with conflicts between liberal and conservative or scientific and religious viewpoints. When doing Parts Work, one recognizes that polarized assertions reflect identification with one of two opposing parts. While such claims may contribute to the larger conversation, they will be partial at best. Miss this essential distinction, and unhelpful—ideological and thus limiting and ultimately dangerous—conclusions result.

Parts Work, when applied at a cultural level, also provides valuable historical insights. Besides helping clarify how Integrative Meta-perspective differs from the cognitive ordering of times past, it also helps us better appreciate the more specific beliefs of previous historical times. We can understand each of history's previously defining cultural narratives in terms of parts-talking-to-parts "cross-talk" between the defining parts of that cultural stage, combined with projection and mythologizing. Direct conversation between parts at a cultural level gave us the easy complementarities of thought found in early cultural realities (think of the yin and yang of Taoist thought or the intertwined serpents of the Greek caduceus), the warring absolutes of medieval belief (setting good clearly against evil, feudal lords solidly separate from peasantry), and with our Modern Age, the juxtapositions of heroic and romantic narratives, the separate-worlds assumptions of Cartesian dualism, and the counterpoised conclusions of liberal and conservative political ideologies. CST argues that each of these parts-talking-to-parts realities in its time served us. Each helped drive the formative dynamics that ordered that period in history as a creative process. But CST also makes clear that parts talking to parts at a cultural level is incompatible with Integrative Meta-perspective and can ultimately only get in the way of going forward (thus Parts Work's third cardinal rule).

Parts Work, done over time, alters not just how a person views specific issues, but also how he or she engages reality more broadly. The work becomes like lifting weights to build the "muscles" of culturally mature capacity. One of the litmus tests for success with this kind of approach is the appearance of culturally mature shifts with regard to questions that the person has not before directly asked.

The same general kind of approach can also be applied to working with more than one person. I often use related methods when assisting groups where issues have become polarized, or with organizations where people wish to address many-sided questions that require careful, in-depth inquiry. When working in this way, I place individuals or small subgroups around the room to represent the various systemic aspects of the question at hand (the various characters/crayons). Another subgroup, seated in a semicircle adjacent to the smaller groups, is assigned the task of engaging these subgroups in conversation to clarify their positions. Later it is the job of this more encompassing group to articulate a larger systemic perspective and explain how that perspective could be translated into right and timely action.

Any at all complete examination of Parts Work would require a book of its own.[1] Here I've included three brief examples. I've chosen these because they are particularly pertinent to understanding Integrative Meta-perspective's big-picture implications. In each case, the person had come to me initially for individual therapy, but the work eventually turned to broader cultural questions and evolved into conversations of a more conceptual sort. I will use the examples not just to illustrate Parts Work, but also to continue the kind of application reflections that I emphasized in the previous chapter and to make further links to earlier theoretical observations. The names are fictitious and the descriptions are necessarily very abbreviated. In each case, they condense conversations that extended over many months.

Stephen—and the Immigration Debate

I'd seen Stephen for several months when he came in for a session following the Thanksgiving holidays. He looked concerned. His family spanned the extremes politically, and the dinner table conversation had become quite heated.

Debate around the immigration question had left Stephen feeling particularly disturbed. Stephen's uncle was very conservative politically

---

1 My upcoming book, *Creative Systems Theory: A Comprehensive Framework for Understanding Purpose, Change, and Interrelationship in Human Systems*, will examine Parts Work in more detail.

and left no doubt that he thought immigration should be severely restricted. Stephen's sister felt just as strongly that immigration benefited the country, and that making citizenship possible for people from other countries, particularly where circumstances in their native countries were troubled, was the only moral thing to do. Stephen's uncle and sister had bumped heads in a major way with neither of them willing to back down.

As Stephen described the scene, I asked him just what about the dinner-table conversation had most bothered him. At first, he thought the answer to my question was obvious—no one would find that degree of conflict in a family a good thing. But with reflection, he saw that his reaction was also more personal. The immigration issue evoked a similar kind of conflict in himself. He could feel his stomach begin to hurt when he thought about it.

Stephen realized that he didn't have good answers for the immigration question, that in fact he had little useful to say about the topic. Particularly given that he was on his town's city council, this was not a small matter. He would clearly need to spend more time with the question and find better ways to think about it than he had found thus far.

After I described how Parts Work provides a simple way to address conflicted issues, Stephen agreed to give it a try. The first part Stephen identified was very much like his uncle—indeed, so much so that Stephen felt a bit embarrassed to own it as a part. It wore a cowboy hat and bordered on being overtly racist. Stephen gave him a chair off to his right.

At least initially, Stephen felt more comfortable with the second part that he identified. It was a college professor and held views more like those of his sister. But as Stephen got more in touch with this second part, he also found himself questioning its conclusions. The professor's views seemed too pat, even arrogant.

In preparation for engaging the parts, Stephen and I talked further about the Parts Work approach. I shared the cardinal rules. I also described how, for him, it appeared that parts had been talking to parts. I suggested that the pain Stephen felt in his stomach was likely a symptom of this internal tension. We talked about how Stephen's first task would be to cut the "wire" between the parts so they would be talking directly to him. His second task would be to talk with each part to find out what it had to contribute, to discern what was helpful and not helpful in what each had to offer.

Stephen went back and forth multiple times, talking first with one part and then the other. Doing so at least helped him begin to appreciate that the immigration question was legitimately complex. Stephen saw that the values expressed by each part were in their own ways valid. Each reflected a kind of good.

His cowboy part talked about pride of place and the importance of protecting community and heritage. It also talked about wanting to be sure there would be good jobs for his daughter and son. It sounded scared, and also angry that what he had worked for might be taken from him and his family.

The professor part, too, voiced values that Stephen could get behind. It spoke about how the U.S. was a country of immigrants and how it was our differences that made us strong. It proposed that immigration was good for the economy, not the reverse. And it made the same moral argument that Stephen's sister had voiced, that taking people in when they are in need is the compassionate thing to do.

But as Stephen spoke with the parts, it became clear to him that each part in its own way also missed the mark. Each left out important pieces of the puzzle and often ended up reaching conclusions that were problematic—and sometimes simply wrong. For example, at one point the more conservative part argued that immigration puts us in danger because such a large portion of immigrants were criminals and even terrorists—an observation that Stephen knew was not supported by the evidence. With similar conviction, the more liberal part at times talked as if having open borders was in and of itself a virtue—a conclusion that Stephen knew came no closer to being the truth and that was in its own way just as dangerous.

At one point, I asked Stephen if his Parts Work conversations were proving helpful. His first response was to express disappointment that not much had changed. He felt no closer to having an answer for the immigration question—indeed, in some ways, he was a lot further from an answer. At least his parts had been sure of their convictions. Conversing with them had left him with an impossibly complex picture of potential benefits and potential harms.

I suggested in response that while Stephen had yet to derive much that could help at the level of policy, in fact there had been change. I asked

him if it wasn't the case that he was seeing things more clearly, better taking everything that needed to be considered into account. He agreed that
he was. I also asked him how his stomach was doing. To his surprise, he
found that it felt considerably better.

As we talked further, I offered to share an experience that had helped
me more usefully frame the immigration debate. A colleague in Europe
had contacted me angrily after reading an article I had written on immigration policy. The dramatic influx of immigrants into his town in
recent years had totally overwhelmed social services and in his view
left little of the town's tradition and history. He had come to regret his
past more liberal feelings about immigration.

I had felt moved by what my colleague had said, but I had also found
myself struck by how different the circumstances were in the state of
Washington where I live. Here, the consequences of recent immigration have been almost entirely positive. We would have neither an apple industry nor a high-tech industry—industries central to my state's
economy and identity—without the contributions of immigrants.

I described to Stephen how surprised my colleague and I had been
with how different the immigration question could seem depending
on the context. We had also been surprised by how much a simple
appreciation for the fact of contextual differences could alter the immigration conversation. I then shared with Stephen an image that later
came to me that had helped me think about the immigration question
in ways that better reflected this more dynamic reality: the image of a
cell's outer membrane. A solid outer membrane is critical to a cell—
without it, life would be impossible. But it is just as critical to the cell's
well-being that the membrane be permeable, that it be able to let in
essential nutrients. The cell's task is to discern the relationship of solid-
ity and permeability that is just right at particular times and places.[2]

Stephen found the image and the more systemic question it pointed toward helpful. It helped him better appreciate how there was no

---

2 Notice how this image helps tie social/political belief together with polarity
   at its most fundamental. I've described how polarity at its most basic juxtaposes difference/distinction and oneness/connectedness. With political
   polarity, conservative belief tends to identify more with boundary and difference ("build the wall"), liberal belief with connectedness and permeability.

one-size-fits-all answer with immigration. But it also helped him better understand that it was possible to arrive at "good enough" answers for particular contexts. Stephen saw that his task, if he was to provide leadership with the immigration question, would be to help his town discern the right balance—the right degree and kind of permeability—for its specific circumstances.

I suggested that Stephen again turn to his parts and articulate his new approach, to make a kind of "leadership statement." He clarified how he saw his task as making this more nuanced kind of discernment. And he shared with his parts that he felt each of them had important input to contribute for this thinking, how each could be a valuable consultant.

Stephen then had an additional recognition that would prove just as important. He saw that he would need more than just these two parts if he was to make decisions most effectively. He needed to have parts that voiced everything that went into creating healthy and vibrant communities. The work Stephen did over the ensuing months helped him both find greater equanimity in himself and be more effective and comfortable in his leadership role with the city council.

May—and the Future of Male/Female Relations

I saw May in therapy several years back. Our work began at a very personal level, but eventually it turned to questions related to changes reshaping how we think about gender and love.

As therapy began, May recounted how intimate relationships in her life had not gone well. She had had one marriage that ended in divorce and a series of intimacies that she felt she had ultimately undermined. She also described how she felt it was time to face what she was pretty sure was the source of the difficulty. She had been repeatedly molested as a young girl by a cousin and had never spoken to anyone about it.

As we began to delve in the history of May's intimate relationships, a common pattern emerged. First, she would be strongly attracted to a man and quickly end up in bed with him. Often these were men who were not good for her and not good to her. Then, after a few months, even if the relationship seemed relatively healthy, she would pick a fight and leave.

In doing Parts Work, the first part May identified was the one that got her so quickly into relationships. It was a young girl who dressed and acted seductively. May talked with this young girl part over several weeks, gradually getting to know her and gaining her trust. May was not sure how she felt about her.

In time, May asked the young girl part what she remembered about the molestation. A couple of things surprised May in hearing the response. First was how the young girl part experienced that it had been her (rather than May) who had been molested. The young girl part was also pretty sure that the molestation had been her fault. At first, she had felt confused and frightened by the older cousin's behavior. But she also described feeling complimented by his attention and over time even being aroused by it. She described feeling that she could not really say no.

May also identified a second part. It had a sword and shield and was dressed for battle. May described feeling that this part had come to the defense of the young girl part. It is this part that had finally said no to the cousin and eventually talked to May's parents about her cousin's behavior. May initially expressed more clearly positive feelings toward this part, but as she got to know it, the picture that emerged also became more complex. Certainly she appreciated that this part had stepped in. But in talking with it in more depth, she realized that it was also this part that was keeping her from getting close even when she met a man who might be good for her.

Over time, May and I spoke together about what needed to happen. She rightly observed that she needed to assure the young girl that the molestation had not been her fault. But I emphasized that May also needed to forgive herself if she personally felt to blame. I described how, just by the way psychological development works, she in her Whole-Person chair would not have been there to protect and intercede at that young age. Once May had forgiven herself, it would then be possible for her to tell the parts that she was sorry that she had not been able to be there for them. She could also commit to them that she would always be there for them in the future.

We also talked about how May would need to be clear with each part that her relationship with it would be changing, fundamentally. No longer would it be acceptable for either of them to take over. And it would certainly not be okay for either part to act on her behalf in the world. The parts could talk with her and share with her what they found important. But it would need to always be her in her Whole-Person chair who had the last word.[3]

Gradually, too, May saw how important it would be that she "cut the wire" that had linked the parts. This took more time to fully grasp, but May came to appreciate how she could understand the constant internal drama and ambivalence that had characterized intimate connectings in her life to that point in terms of cross-talk between these conflicting parts.

Eventually, May had more specific conversations with each part. In talking with the little girl, along with assuring the little girl that she was not to blame for what had happened, May was also able to clarify that the fact that she liked closeness was ultimately a good thing. But May also made clear that going forward it would need to be her in her Whole-Person chair, not the little girl, who decided when closeness in the world was appropriate. May was also able to clarify something further for the little girl that would ultimately be key. She described how while relating to a man could not provide completion for the little girl, there was a kind of closeness that would be essential for her well-being: her relationship with May in the Whole-Person chair.

In talking with the warrior part, May affirmed that she was grateful that it had provided protection in the past. But she also made clear that protecting was now her task. The warrior part could tap her on the shoulder if it felt things might not be safe. But from now on, it would be May's job in her Whole-Person chair to determine when things were safe and to decide appropriate action if they were not.

Work with these often past-related and more internal dynamics took several months. But eventually our conversation turned to the future and the question of just what relating to a man from her chair might look like. The first thing that May saw was that doing so would require more patience, that it would necessarily involve knowing both

---

3   A subtle distinction underlies the second cardinal rule. Ultimately, the issue is not so much that problems arise when parts have relationships with the world but that parts have never really been capable of having relationships with the world. Parts have only been capable of mythologized fantasies about the world. In another way, we recognize how Integrative Meta-perspective is simply about seeing life more accurately.

herself and the man she was with more deeply than with intimacy as she had known it. She also saw that love of this sort was probably going to have less drama. We talked about how she might need to grieve some of the reliable intensities of times past and be okay with love feeling more ordinary.

These observations eventually opened up a deeper conversation about how love in our time is changing. I was surprised at just how far this further conversation was able to go. It started with looking at some of the practical skills required to make Whole-Person relationships work. I offered that in the end it all came down to clear yeses and nos. The nos started within herself. She needed to make clear nos to each of her parts in the sense of her always being in charge. But she also needed to be sure she was making clear boundaries in the world so that men did not misunderstand her intent. And she needed to be comfortable saying her nos emphatically if that was what was required.

As far as yeses, May saw that she needed to draw on what each part could contribute. And May made a further yes-related observation that began to take the conversation to a different level. She asked whether, if what we were talking about was really going to work, she wouldn't also need to be more overt in expressing her "yeses" to the man.

I offered that I thought this observation was very insightful. We talked about how historically it has been the man's job to do the pursuing, with the woman often playing "hard to get." In the old picture, men expected to hear nos, and sometimes repeated nos, particularly from women who wanted to be seen as virtuous or particularly desirable. May saw that if she wanted men to take her nos seriously, they needed to be real nos. But she also saw that it was just as important that she be willing to clearly communicate "yes" if that was what she was choosing. She needed to take a more explicit kind of responsibility in intimacy. She really couldn't have it both ways.

With these reflections, we had taken important steps toward grasping what love, and relationships between the sexes more generally, might look like in a culturally mature reality. It is a complex topic, but it is also true that we can sum up much of what is needed going forward in terms of being more clear and conscious with our yeses and nos. May and I talked together about the radical implications of doing so, both for relationship and for coming to hold identity in more powerful and complete ways.[4]

Eventually, May again turned to more personal questions, now about the kinds of choices she wanted to make going forward. As she worked, she found the two parts that she had previously identified evolving, more and more becoming voices in herself she could rely on in making good decisions. Using that language of yeses and nos, the little girl part gradually matured into an advocate for not being afraid of saying yes when that was what was true. The warrior part came to look less fierce, but at the same time became an even more uncompromising advocate for making good boundaries.[5] Over time, May also added further parts that could help her in living the most caring and effective life.

Mark—and the Larger Relationship of the Spiritual and the Material

Mark came to me after several years as director of a local retreat center. He had become unhappy with his effectiveness as a leader. He described laying out plans, then questioning himself and not following through. He was sure he had the capacity to do better. Mark also found himself baffled as to just what it would mean to provide useful direction for the organization. Some relationships within the organization had become conflicted, and it was not at all clear to him what being a good leader would entail.

After briefly introducing Parts Work, I had Mark identify the part that he felt was getting in the way. At first, he had a hard time visualizing it. It would show up as a vague outline, almost ghostlike, then as quickly disappear. I asked Mark how he felt about the part. He responded that while he would like to see it more clearly, he had basically good feelings toward it. He recognized that it somehow had special importance to him.

---

4 *On the Evolution of Intimacy: A Brief Exploration into the Past, Present, and Future of Gender and Love* examines needed new skills and awarenesses in depth and also offers more intimacy- and gender-related Parts Work examples.

5 Notice how this emphasis on clear yeses and nos in another way brings us back to the two halves of polarity at its most fundamental. Nos are about difference, and yeses are about connectedness. Culturally mature relationship requires that we learn to honor each more consciously and act on each more explicitly.

I suggested that we move on and get other parts into the room. Mark brought in a more intellectual part—he had gotten his undergraduate degree in philosophy. He also identified a more creative part and a part that particularly enjoyed being in nature. To his surprise, in addition, he brought in a more scientific part. His dad had been a scientist, but he had never thought of himself that way. Mark took time to get to know each of these additional parts.

I then asked Mark what parts he most drew on when he led. He realized that in various ways each part helped out. But he also recognized that the part he had initially identified played an especially strong role, particularly with his leadership at the retreat center. It was obvious that we needed to learn more about it.

When Mark turned to the part this time, the image was more clear. He was a Buddhist monk, sitting cross-legged in contemplation. Again, Mark observed that he liked the part. He also observed that it had probably been that part that had gotten him to take the job at the center. The retreat center was best known for programs that supported beliefs of either a spiritual/New Age or liberal/progressive sort.

I reminded Mark that he had initially identified that part as a problem and suggested that he talk with the part about his concerns. After turning to the monk and sharing with him what he had told me about not following through, Mark asked the monk what he knew about what was going on. He then went over to the monk's chair.

At first, the monk just kept on with his meditating. Then finally he looked up at Mark and said, "Why are you talking to me about this? Leading is your job. I'm doing mine."

Mark initially found this exchange odd, but it soon began to make sense. He saw that when he was in a leadership role, very often he would end up sitting in the monk's chair—or the monk would slip into his—he couldn't tell quite which. Given that the organization he was leading was a spiritual organization, the fact that the monk might be in charge at first seemed reasonable. But Mark now realized that this ghostlike monk didn't have the skills needed for leadership. And the monk quite obviously didn't want the job.

Mark spent the next several sessions exploring what leading more specifically from his chair might look like. He saw that doing so would at the least challenge him to be more visible as a leader, to take more

overt responsibility in the organization's functioning. He also recognized that such leadership would somehow require him to draw
on the strengths of all of his parts in making decisions. We talked at
some length about both what good leadership has always asked and
also about the new skills and capacities needed for effective leadership in our time.

At one point, I suggested to Mark that he choose a specific leadership challenge as a way to practice applying these observations. Mark
decided to work on the conflicted relationship he had mentioned. It
would sorely test his as-yet fledgling understanding of Whole-Person/
Whole-System leadership.

An employee of the organization who people generally liked had
been stealing petty cash. She had also not been doing her job and was
behaving in ways that were doing harm to the morale of people working with her. Mark recognized that it could very well be important for
the well-being of the organization that she be let go. But he had also
found it very hard to take the steps necessary to do so.

The situation had been made more difficult by the reactions of the
organization's board. The board would need to approve the decision,
and they found the idea of dismissing someone even harder than he
did. The situation had very much become a double bind. Mark could
keep the woman on with considerable—perhaps even terminal—long-
term damage to the organization. Or he could have her released, with
the resulting feelings of guilt in the organization in their own way potentially putting the organization at risk. There was no obvious right
answer.

I suggested that Mark bring all of his parts into the room and get
their opinions on what he should do. Mark first asked the monk. But
the monk could only speak about forgiveness and love. He could not
support firing the woman. All of the other parts, in contrast, concluded
that doing anything else would be shirking his responsibility as a leader.
The result of doing nothing might be short-term peace. But in the longer term, the organization's contribution would be compromised.

As Mark agonized over his decision, I shared an observation that I
had had in working with other organizations. I described how the kind of
dilemma he confronted was common with more spiritual and liberal organizations—put more conceptually, with groups that identify with more

left-hand, archetypally feminine, oneness-associated parts. When difference and distinction is needed, such organizations have a hard time responding effectively. And the anti-authoritarian beliefs that commonly accompany such identification can directly undermine the exercising of leadership. Often, the result is that such organizations simply fail.

Mark saw both how difficult a position he was in and also how important it would be for him to act decisively. He was going to need to take a stand, one that was likely not going to be popular. Indeed, it might result in him having to step down from his leadership role. But he saw too that if he was going to act in ways that would ultimately most benefit the organization—really be a leader—this is what he would have to do.

Taking on this often wrenching leadership challenge in time opened a deeper conversation. Mark had seen that it didn't work for the monk in him to lead—that it was a part. The recognition that the organization's identification with a related part undermined its effectiveness was now making him question the underlying beliefs that defined its mission. He saw that if the organization wanted to provide leadership for humanity's future—as it claimed to be doing—something more was needed. And at some level he recognized that the needed "more" would be fundamentally disruptive.

It was the start of an exchange that would stretch out over many months and have us grappling with some of life's biggest questions. Mark commented that he had read some of what I had written about how the concept of Cultural Maturity challenges us to rethink both religion and science. He wondered if at some level that wasn't the challenge he was confronting. Certainly, his circumstance provided a good place to see just why needed changes might be important, at least for the more spirituality/religion side of things.

We talked about how, from the vantage of Integrative Meta-perspective, both spirituality and religion as we conventionality think of them, and science, at least of the mechanistic sort, stop being about truth in a last-word sense. Using the box-of-crayons metaphor, they become crayons. In Parts Work terms, they reflect parts—characters—as opposed to the Whole-Person/Whole-System chair. Historically, we've either made one or the other the whole of truth, or given each a part of truth in some form of separate-worlds dualism.

Mark said he wanted to take the conversation further, look more specifically at how CST provides a more encompassing picture. I agreed, but cautioned that it could only be a brief glimpse into a much larger inquiry. I asked Mark if he understood the general way a creative frame redefines the science/religion debate. To summarize, I reminded him of how polarity at its most fundamental juxtaposes difference/distinction on one hand with unity/connectedness on the other. And I laid out how, framed creatively, science and religion reflect these complementary creative ingredients, expressed as extremes and at the largest of systemic scales. Science is about collective right-hand, archetypally masculine experience—the difference/distinction half of ultimate polarity—cleansed of contamination by the left.[6] Religion is about collective left-hand, archetypally feminine sensibility—ultimate polarity's unity/connectedness dimension—in its purest manifestation.[7]

In response to Mark's continued questioning, I briefly filled out how historical perspective supports this picture. I described how the kinds of stories scientific and spiritual beliefs have drawn on (from the animistic to the humanistic and rationalistic), the kinds of imagery they have referenced (from the creaturely, to the magical and mythic, to figures who mirror ourselves and a world pictured as separate and objective), and the general kinds of behaviors that they imply are societally appropriate and morally acceptable, can each be understood to follow predictably from how more right-hand and more left-hand sensibilities manifest with each of culture's creative stages. We see this creatively ordered progression in science's evolution from the nature-centered beliefs of tribal times, to more philosophically idealist sorts of understanding (as

---

6 Science is about distinction—this as opposed to that. Biology differentiates the creaturely into taxonomies of genus and species, chemistry gives us the periodic table and delineates the workings of atoms and molecules, and classical physics gives us the this-versus-that laws of material cause and effect.

7 We can think of religious belief, wherever we find it, in terms of four connectedness-related themes: how things arose from the undivided ("in the beginning"), community (congregation and communion), right thought and behavior (shared moral assumptions), and how experiences interrelate (and, in the end, how it all interrelates). In Latin, *re-ligare*, the root of the word "religion," means "to connect." William James put it this way: "In mystic states we both become one with the Absolute and we become aware of our oneness."

with Aristotle's notion of an "unmoved mover"), to views in the Middle Ages that postulated mystically infused forces (as with alchemy), to the scientific method and its formalization with modern age understanding. We witness this same progression in another way with religion's evolution from animism, to polytheism, to absolutist monotheism, to the more liberal monotheism of the Reformation.

Eventually, I made an observation that makes no sense when viewed from how we usually think but that follows directly from this creative interpretation. In spite of how often through history the relationship between science and religion has appeared adversarial, science and religion have all along been engaged in an essential kind of conspiracy. And I suggested a conversation topic that would need to wait for another time. Integrative Meta-perspective not only offers that we might see a larger picture, it makes it possible to entertain more dynamic and complete understandings of both science and spirituality.[8]

As Mark and I turned more specifically to his efforts with the retreat center, I realized that one additional conceptual piece that followed from where Integrative Meta-perspective takes us could be important for his considerations. We talked some about the Dilemma of Trajectory, and with this, an important way its implications could be misinterpreted. Given that people in our time have become so distanced from the more archetypally feminine aspects of life, sensibilities that we have often most known through spiritual experience, a person could assume that anything that affirms these parts of experience would be helpful. But not everything that makes such links benefits us, at least not without significant added perspective.

I think, for example, of the referencing by certain groups of beliefs and practices from earlier historical times. Previously I've noted such referencing with the ideas of classical Eastern philosophy and Native American teachings. But different groups can do something similar with the fundamentalist, monotheistic spiritual beliefs of medieval and early modern age times. Such drawing of parallels can provide impor-

---

8 In *Cultural Maturity: A Guidebook for the Future*, I address how our understandings of science and religion change when viewed through a culturally mature lens. I also address what the implications might be for the future of each of them.

tant insight and help reestablish connections that have been lost. But it is important that we not confuse the beliefs and practices of times past with what is required today. Going back, however pleasant and seemingly affirming the experience, is ultimately regression. And regression can't get us where we need to go.

Mark acknowledged that this was in fact a familiar trap with thinking in his organization. We talked some about blindnesses that we might expect to see with this lack of perspective. We also talked about leadership challenges that falling for this kind of trap would necessarily present.

But it was time to get back to Parts Work. Now that Mark had a clearer picture of the role that spiritual/religious experience might play in Integrative Meta-perspective's more whole-box-of-crayons picture, he could more effectively address the concrete choices he needed to make going forward. He had questions not just about what being an effective leader for the organization would require, but also about whether the organization was in fact engaged in work that he could get behind. He didn't have final answers on either count. But he recognized that, with Parts Work, he now had a method that could help him find the direction in which he needed to go. He again turned to his various parts, now using them as consultants as he attempted to piece together just what might come next.

C H A P T E R   S I X

Creative Systems Theory... and a Couple of Ultimate Human Questions

A particularly consequential way that Integrative Meta-perspective helps us as we look to the future has been suggested throughout this book's reflections. Along with providing a new kind of cultural narrative and making available new skills and capacities, Cultural Maturity's cognitive changes make possible new frameworks for understanding. Integrative Meta-perspective's more whole-box-of-crayons systemic vantage invites conceptual approaches that before now would have made no sense to us.

This further contribution has been most explicit when I have drawn on ideas from Creative Systems Theory. CST offers big-picture, long-term, multidisciplinary perspective for addressing human systems. The theory makes sense only from the vantage of Integrative Meta-perspective. Ultimately, we can think of CST's ideas as following directly from it. Once we recognize that intelligence has multiple aspects that work together to support our toolmaking, meaning-making, "creative" capacities, there is an important sense in which CST is a natural result.

CST offers a way to bring new dynamism and nuance to how we understand both ourselves and the larger world around us. Through applying a creative frame, CST's thinking highlights the fact that we are alive, and human. Ideas like those of CST take on particular significance with the recognition, central to this inquiry, that the most important questions of our time are questions of value, and in the end, questions of how we understand. Think of CST as a toolbox of culturally mature concepts.

Here we address CST more specifically. This can necessarily be but the briefest of introductions.[1] Following some lickety-split overview observations, I will turn to a particularly provocative implication of how CST alters understanding that provides important support for the theory's larger significance. A creative frame lets us address questions that always before have left us baffled.

Creative Systems Theory

CST's approach is not the only way to derive new ways of thinking from Integrative Meta-perspective's changes, but it could well prove to be of particular importance. In an earlier footnote, I proposed that the notion that intelligence is creatively ordered has major significance in the history of ideas. As with how the introduction of the clockworks metaphor presaged the thinking of the Modern Age, it invites us to entertain a new kind of fundamental organizing concept. Because a creative frame puts the human story as a whole in larger perspective, it could be argued that the leap in understanding it produces is of even greater significance than that which gave us modern age thought. If CST had been around before civilization's rise—which it obviously could not have been—it would have predicted at least the general contours of both the modern age worldview and the worldviews of each of the major periods in culture's evolution that preceded it.

CST reflects a sort of thinking that hasn't before been possible and that would not before have seemed to be necessary. Because a creative frame inherently "bridges" the conceptual polarities of times past, CST ideas reflect the dynamism of human experience in ways that familiar modern age ways of understanding cannot.[2] CST applies three kinds

---

1   I have written about CST concepts and their application extensively in other sources. See in particular the Creative Systems Theory website (www.CSThome.org), the teaching resource *Pattern and Reality,* and *Cultural Maturity: A Guidebook for the Future (with an Introduction to the Ideas of Creative Systems Theory).* My next book will be a comprehensive work on CST and its implications.

2   I've described how a creative frame reconciles the Dilemma of Differentiation. It propels us beyond both the difference-identifying conclusions of rationalist/scientific thought and the unity-identifying con-

of patterning notions in making distinctions: Patterning in Time, Patterning in Space, and Whole-System Patterning Concepts. With each, the new kind of understanding it represents has now become essential.

CST Patterning in Time distinctions have had a central place in these reflections. They've given us the developmental notions that I've drawn on in proposing parallels between different scales of human formation processes—from a creative act, to personal psychological development, to the growth of a relationship or organization, to the evolution of culture. One of the best places to recognize the importance of Pattering in Time concepts is with how CST rewrites history, makes the past about much more than just a chronicling of events and inventions. Patterning in Time at a cultural scale addresses the evolution of human narrative, both the human narrative as a whole and also the different forms that the human narrative has taken at different times and places. Events come to make deeper sense and history becomes much more dynamic, and as inquiry, more rich and compelling.[3]

Just as much, Patterning in Time concepts applied at a cultural level have essential big-picture implications for addressing the future. We can use them, as we have here, to help us make sense of the times we live in and to prepare for what times ahead may ask of us. They help us understand the challenges before us not just in terms of technological advancement, but also in terms of the values, skills, and ways of understanding that will be necessary to a future that is imbued with creativity and purpose.

Patterning in Time notions at a cultural scale also have more immediate leadership applications. Effective decision-making in a globalized world becomes very difficult without an understanding of temporal

---

clusions of more romantic/spiritual belief. In the process, it offers the possibility of understanding in ways that not only highlight the fact that we are alive, but that place that which makes us particular as living beings forefront.

3   Patterning in Time observations let us make much finer historical distinctions than those that I've drawn on in this book. For example, they identify approximately one hundred-year substages within modern age culture and also smaller cycles that happen over a span of decades. See *Cultural Maturity: A Guidebook for the Future*.

context, an appreciation for the times in culture's developmental story in which events reside. In my book *Cultural Maturity*, I make reference to how the belief of George W. Bush at the beginning of the second Iraq War that the Iraqi people would celebrate U.S. intervention makes no sense with any understanding of cultural stage differences.

CST Patterning in Space notions address more here-and-now systemic relationships. We can think of the box-of-crayons image as a Patterning in Space metaphor. I've described how we can better understand the relationships between conflicting ideological views, such as those of the political left and the political right, by thinking of them as opposing systemic "crayons"—a Patterning in Space observation. Relationships between disciplines in a university or departments in a company can in a similar way be thought of as Patterning in Space relationships. Thus far, CST Patterning in Space thinking has been most developed with the theory's framework for understanding personality style differences—the Creative Systems Personality Typology. The CSPT shines a light on how remarkably different we can be from one another as a product of temperament. The framework makes a major original contribution.[4]

It is reasonable to ask why we most often fail to recognize personality style differences that can seem so obviously important on close examination. We encounter such blindness even with people for whom a sensitivity to the depths of such differences would seem essential— such as teachers, psychologists, and physicians. CST proposes that the explanation is the same as that we encountered in wondering why we have not before seen more systemic understandings of history—we need the more conscious engagement with our multiple ways of knowing that Integrative Meta-perspective makes possible for temperament differences to make full sense. The Creative Systems Personality Typology describes how temperament differences, in a way similar to what we find with developmental stages, reflect the preferential influence of different intelligences (or again, more accurately, of different relationships of intelligences).

---

4 See the short book *The Power of Diversity: An Introduction to the Creative Systems Personality Typology* or the Creative Systems Personality Typology webpage (www.CSPTHome.org)

Whole-System Patterning Concepts are just what they sound like. They bring together everything that at any moment makes something true. I've implied Whole System patterning distinctions in emphasizing the importance of getting beyond outdated absolutist moral dictates and thinking more directly in terms of what makes an act moral. Or, instead of moral, we could say the degree an act is creative or generative (or simply whether it makes us "more").

CST identifies two main kinds of Whole-System Patterning Concepts. The first addresses truth in a way that is at once most bare-boned and most encompassing. I was drawing on it in Chapter One when I observed that good decision-making necessarily starts with asking the pertinent Question of Referent. I went on to describe how culturally mature decision-making requires that we draw on referents of a more specifically integrative, whole-box-of-crayons systemic sort. Formally, CST uses the term Integrative Referent to describe this first kind of Whole-System Patterning Concept.[5]

More informally, because in applying such referents we are attempting to get at what will produce the most ultimately life-enhancing choices, CST often refers to this kind of measure simply as "aliveness." Framed more in terms of change, it describes the "creative edge" of understanding as it applies to a particular issue or system. This first kind of Whole-System discernment assumes an ultimately embracing kind of importance in our time with the challenge of rethinking wealth and progress. In a new, more complete sense, our definitions of larger significance must be affirming of life and effectively address what, as humans, is creatively possible.

The second Whole-System Patterning Concept, what CST calls Capacitance, is more specifically quantitative. Capacitance refers to the amount of life a system can tolerate before it becomes too much— think of a balloon that, if filled too full, might break. One of the lessons

---

5   Referents of times past have most often associated final truth with one aspect of systemic complexity. We've seen this in modern times, for example, with making money our defining measure for wealth and IQ our bottom line for intelligence.

that people doing Parts Work find most powerful and useful concerns Capacitance. Living from that Whole-Person chair requires that a person structure his or her life in ways that honor Capacitance limits. It follows from how systemic dynamics work that if the demands of a person's life regularly exceed the person's available Capacitance, parts will step in to protect the person from being overwhelmed. In speaking of how current cultural challenges can result in Transitional Absurdities and regression, I was describing what predictably happens if the exceptional demands of today's human circumstances threaten to exceed the Capacitance we as a species have to deal with them.

As with Patterning in Time and Patterning in Space notions, Whole-System Patterning Concepts become possible only with Integrative Meta-perspective. Engaging questions as systemic wholes requires that we draw on the whole of ourselves as systems. On first encountering CST, people tend to think of Patterning in Time and Patterning in Space concepts as most striking and obviously new. But with familiarity, it is often Whole-System Patterning Concepts that people find most significant. At least they tend to find them most immediately practical as tools in their daily lives.

Proceeding successfully once we are past Cultural Maturity's threshold requires each of these three kinds of discernments. Each is fundamentally new in the kind of concept it represents. CST's approach is not the only way to make such distinctions. But the theory, by offering a sophisticated, culturally mature toolbox that effectively addresses all of them, can get us a long way with the leadership tasks ahead.

Answering Ultimate Questions

One of the most intriguing consequences of Integrative Meta-perspective, particularly when we add CST's creative frame, is that it lets us address questions that in times past have either left us baffled or produced limited, ultimately unhelpful answers. Earlier chapters in the book have provided a glimpse. I've touched on an array of topics with arguably "ultimate" implications, such as the origins of war, the nature of human purpose, and how leadership, love, and identity will each ask new things of us in times ahead. In the previous chapter, I touched on an even more big-picture ultimate concern in beginning to address how we might best think about a larger relationship between science and religion. Such topics were the focus of my 2016 book, *Quick and Dirty Answers to the Biggest of Questions: Creative Systems Theory Explains What It Is All About (Really)*.[6]

As a way to conclude the book's reflections, here I will take on a couple of further, particularly provocative ultimate concerns: the seeming contradiction between free will and determinism, and how best to think about existence's workings as a whole, including our place in them. Each topic provides further evidence for both the newness of the kind of thinking Integrative Meta-perspective represents and the particular significance of a creative frame. We will see how addressing either question—indeed, just framing either of them in useful ways—requires applying systemic understanding of the more dynamic and complete, all-the-crayons-in-the-box sort that becomes possible only with Integrative Meta-perspective. We will also see how a creative frame provides a concise and nuanced way to do so. In each case, Integrative Meta-perspective, when combined with CST's particular approach to understanding, reveals new kinds of answers. And in each case, the "new common sense" quality of the answers helps affirm at least their general rightness.

Free Will and Determinism

The seeming contradiction between free will and determinism befuddles thinkers from every realm it touches—psychology, philosophy, religion, science. Within the modern age worldview's mechanistic, simple cause-and-effect reality, free will makes no sense. The idea at best becomes fantasy. Yet we experience ourselves as choosing freely. Indeed, we identify with this fact and celebrate the ability to do so with ever greater freedom as one of the great achievements of the Modern Age.

If we think at all deeply (at least if we make use of Integrative Meta-perspective in doing the thinking), we recognize that neither picture really holds up. The person who writes lengthy volumes to disprove free will certainly hopes that the act of writing is in some way a product of choice. He or she also hopes that the effort will affect the choices of others. And

---

6   Charles M. Johnston, MD, *Quick and Dirty Answers to the Biggest of Questions: Creative Systems Theory Explains What It Is All About (Really)*, ICD Press, Seattle, 2016.

any person who looks at all closely at free will recognizes that our choices are always limited by multiple outside constraints and that much that is most important in our decision-making has unconscious origins.

Notions that have been central in this book's reflections point toward the needed larger picture. Our box-of-crayons metaphor at least suggests the importance of something more. Put simply, determinism and free will—or rather, our beliefs about them—become crayon-specific notions. As such, we would expect neither by itself, nor even the two as conventionally conceived in combination, to get us where we need to go. And the way Cultural Maturity's cognitive changes redefine awareness's role begins to bring the needed larger picture into focus. Integrative Meta-perspective affirms that conscious awareness is real and important. But it also suggests that the way we have thought about conscious awareness—tied to rationality and giving us from-a-balcony objectivity—has stopped short of its ultimate significance. Integrative Meta-perspective describes a role for conscious awareness that is more powerful in all that it draws on. But in confronting inherent limits to what conscious awareness can know, it is also more humble. If we appreciate deeply how this picture is different, we come a long way toward reconciling the free will/determinism debate.

The reflections that follow are adapted from a 2018 article I titled "Come On, Stephen Hawking: The Quandary of Free Will in an Apparently Deterministic Universe." I wrote it after watching physicist Stephen Hawking's public television series "Genius." The series took on a variety of intriguing questions, from the possibility of time travel to how, as humans, we got here—to the apparent contradiction between free will and determinism. The first section below quotes directly from my earlier article as a way of bringing attention to the significance of the determinism/free will quandary and the challenge that attempting to reconcile it presents. I will then turn to observations that fill out how a more "creative" understanding of the workings of cognition helps us get beyond it.

From "Come On, Stephen Hawking"

Physicist Stephen Hawking introduced his recent series on public television with the claim that he would show how ordinary people, just by looking closely, can make sense of ultimate questions. I applaud the effort. Much in the series provided useful information. And I have immense respect for Hawking's contributions to physics.

That said, I was frequently disappointed. Often, I found myself responding "Come on, Stephen. You can do better than that." What Hawking's assertions often most made clear is that physics to this point, even at its best, is unable to help us with really ultimate concerns. This was certainly the case with his episode on free will.

We can miss how deeply the experience of free will challenges usual understanding. Free will and determinism each seem self-evident. But as we conventionally think of them, they present mutually exclusive realities. Whether our experience of free will can be reconciled with science's picture of a deterministic world represents one of modern understanding's great quandaries.

Hawking claims to successfully answer the question, but I found his explanation unsatisfying. At best it was unnecessarily complicated. More, I think it was simply wrong. Appreciating what was missing in his explanation offers valuable insight into how contemporary understanding more generally often stops short. It also sheds valuable light on what a needed next chapter in human understanding asks of us and makes possible.

Hawking introduces his examination of the free will/determinism dilemma with the familiar tale of Newton's apple. He notes that Newton's laws of motion give us a deterministic—mechanistic, cause-and-effect—universe. He cites 18th-century French scholar Pierre-Simon Laplace's often-quoted claim that if we knew the position and velocity of every object in the universe, we could predict the whole of future events. He then correctly observes that if Newton's picture is right and complete, free will is necessarily an illusion.

Hawking then describes an experiment from cognitive science that he claims demonstrates this illusion at work. In the experiment, subjects are first wired up to an EEG machine (which measures brain waves). A large red button is then placed before each subject. The subjects are instructed to hit the button whenever they choose. The results contradict what we might expect. The EEG readings demonstrate that we see evidence of "choice" (in the form of observable brain wave activity) well before the subjects hit the button (consciously make the choice).

I included the word "claims" in the previous paragraph because of how Hawking interprets the results of this experiment. Hawking proposes that the body is 'a complex machine' that works according to the deterministic laws of a Newtonian world. From this, he concludes that because the subject's actions were seen first in their bodies (in the EEG recordings), what they experienced as "choice" was in fact predetermined and thus not free will at all.

Having boxed himself into a corner if he is going to do anything more than side with determinism, Hawking then gives himself some wiggle room. It is good that he does, since it is hard to imagine Hawking making the effort to develop this series—and certainly to live the courageous and creative life that he has—if he did not believe at some level that his choices could alter outcomes.

Hawking describes how modern advances add an important further layer of complexity to classical physics' deterministic picture. Quantum mechanics—which functions at the level of the very small—requires that we include uncertainty in our understanding of the physical universe. (Those who have taken a physics class will remember Schrödinger's cat.) Hawking proposes that we best think of existence as having two layers that work according to wholly different rules: a subatomic world ordered by "random" processes, and our more everyday world that follows the deterministic rules of simple cause and effect. The fact that this way of thinking introduces uncertainty into the equation at least opens the door to the possibility that we might bridge the previously irreconcilable assumptions of free will and determinism. But this two-world explanation only opens the door a crack. And Hawking's next demonstration illustrates that for him it does so in only a trivial way.

Hawking uses a simple apparatus—one with an upper and a lower chamber—to demonstrate how he sees the relationship between these two kinds of determination. The lower chamber contains a radioactive element—a substance that decays according to the indeterminate mechanisms of quantum mechanics. The upper chamber holds a catapult that launches a projectile on a pre-established (Newtonian) path once its mechanism is triggered. Subatomic particles released from the lower compartment do the triggering. Hawking proposes that this two-step mechanism accurately describes how things in the real world work. Quantum mechanical randomness gets things started. After this, events follow the laws of classical determinism.

The demonstration is fine to a point, and is consistent with physics' current consensus narrative, but it stops short if our interest is free will. Two related recognitions are key to understanding just how. First, as long as we remain in a mechanistic reality, the apparent paradox of free will and determinism will remain a paradox. "Random" processes, like deterministic process, are fully consistent with a mechanistic worldview. And second, random processes tell us nothing about will in any directed sense. Thus, while Hawking's apparatus may defy prediction, it again tells us little that helps us with the free will/determinism quandary. Hawking's description leaves us with an "explanation" that, while superficially accurate, explains very little.

Hawking concludes by proposing an additional mechanism that he claims puts the free will/determinism question to rest once and for all. It draws on the idea from contemporary physics that there is not just one universe, but an infinite number of parallel universes. Hawking takes this 'multiverse' hypothesis as fact. He argues that "parallel universes are more than a theory. I believe

they are inevitable." And he puts it forward as an ultimate explanation for free will. In his words, "Everything does happen, just in
another universe."

Again we find an "explanation" that, even if it holds up, fails to
address the free-will-versus-determinism paradox in any convincing way. In other writings I describe how, while the notion of an
infinite number of universes may prove accurate, there are very
good reasons to question it.[7] For now it is enough to note that
drawing on the multiverse hypothesis makes for an inordinately
complicated way to answer the free will/determinism question.
Culturally mature perspective suggests that we can address it in
ways that are straightforward—even simple.

Further Observations: Free Will, Conscious Awareness,
and the Life of the Body

To begin to get at the possibility of simpler explanation, we can return to the important recognition that Hawking illustrated with his
EEG demonstration—that the conscious experience of choice can be a
secondary phenomenon. Hawking interprets this recognition to mean
that choice is a product of deterministic, mechanical processes. In his
words: "Brain is made of matter, which must follow the laws of nature.
There is no ghost in the machine."

Creative Systems Theory concurs that there is no "ghost" (a reference to some separate subjective counterpart to the body's objective
workings). But in agreeing with this assertion, it is not taking sides
in the objective-versus-subjective debate. Rather, it is arguing for the
importance of thinking in ways that are more encompassing and complete—more systemic.

In the end, Hawking's interpretation of his EEG demonstration
reflects limited understandings of both how the body functions and
the nature of conscious awareness. The questions raised by a related
"thought experiment" help illustrate. Imagine a gifted football running
back rapidly cutting this way and that as he makes his way down the
field. A close look reveals that the running back's cuts are taking place

---

7 See *Cultural Maturity: A Guidebook for the Future.*

more quickly, and in ways that are more complex and subtle, than could ever happen by consciously choosing them one at a time. The conscious aspects of awareness simply aren't built to function that rapidly.

Does this mean, then, that the running back is not choosing? And, more specifically, does it mean that, because his body moves before he "chooses," that what we witness is nothing more than mechanical—and thus deterministic—reflex? Even if we include Hawking's addition of quantum mechanical "randomness," we find ourselves with a less than convincing picture that only raises more questions. For example, are the outcomes of games then predetermined—or, alternatively, perhaps random? Either way, we are left wondering why we would attend a football game—and perhaps feeling a bit duped. I think in fact it is the explanation that is ultimately silly. Clearly in the running back's movements we witness something that is not just vital, but profoundly so.

CST provides a more conceptually demanding—but also more elegant—interpretation. It starts with the recognition that more sophisticated ways of thinking about the body and about conscious awareness are not just possible, but necessary, if we are to be at all complete in our understanding. As far as the body, the theory offers an expressly more systemic picture of what it means to be embodied. We come to see the body not as a separate machine, but as an integral part of who we are as dynamic, living—and specifically human—beings. We appreciate how body sensibilities represent one part of intelligence's larger complexity. Is it not obvious that what we so delight in in the running back's movements is "intelligent"?

CST also alters how we think about conscious awareness. Traditionally we have thought of conscious awareness as who we are—captain of the cellular ship. I've described how this kind of identification reached an extreme with modern age thought. Objective then became wholly separate from subjective and gradually assumed the mantel of final truth. At the same time, individual identity became associated almost wholly with conscious awareness. In the modern age picture, we *are* conscious awareness; we *have* a body.

How deeply the past's outmoded picture of conscious awareness now fails us has been one of the key contributions of modern psychology and psychiatry. In his classic book *Man and His Symbols*, psychiatrist Carl Jung challenged our modern age interpretation with these words:

"Where there is a will there is a way is the superstition of modern man." He went on to observe that "what we commonly call 'self-knowledge' is a very limited knowledge."[8] Integrative Meta-perspective makes clear that not only does thinking of free will as free and willful in the unfettered sense implied by our modern age picture leave us short, in the end it translates into but another kind of determinism. It is just that with this kind of determinism it is we (in our identification with conscious awareness) who get to do the determining.

A Creative Frame

CST's evolutionary framing of history alerts us to the fact that the free-will-versus-determinism debate has been a product of a developmentally understandable, but systemically incomplete view of the world. As we have experienced the debate, it has been based on a falsely framed dichotomy, a juxtaposing of alternative determinisms, neither of which ultimately holds up. Each determinism has served in similar ways to protect us—as polar explanations of every sort do—from life's ultimately rich, but also easily overwhelming uncertainties and complexities. And as with other polarized explanations, today each equally leaves us short.

At first glance, neither side in the free-will-versus-determinism debate may like the results with CST's reformulation. Viewed through a creative lens, free will becomes not only less free, but also less ours to direct, than those of an individualistic bent might prefer. And neither is determination as predetermined as advocates of either a more scientific determinism or the determinisms of religious faith might wish. Whichever side of the debate we identify with, we confront that change involves multiple, systemically related factors and that uncertainty in some way always intrudes. Of particular importance, one of those factors is always ourselves. We can't escape—as physics has well demonstrated—that the state of the observer affects the act of observing. Like it or not, limits always play a role.

But at the same time, the outcome on both fronts when viewed through a creative lens becomes ultimately more profound. While free will loses the absoluteness of its freedom, at once it becomes even more radically significant and arguably more powerful in its effect. Free will's function in

---

8 Carl Jung, *Man and His Symbols*, Dell, 1968.

a creative picture is to serve as a catalyst and a spark in the creative mechanisms that ultimately make us who we are. Those who identify with the free will side of the equation might fear a loss of control. But in the end, the result is a more "experimental" kind of control that, as we look to the future, provides not only many more options but also options that will be more ultimately consequential. Control in this larger sense also continually affirms what ultimately makes it meaningful to be human.

On the determinism side of the equation, while traditional causalities of all sorts stop being as clear-cut as we have thought them to be, at the same time complexity's picture becomes more dramatically multifaceted and change takes on a new, more dynamic significance. Those who identity with determinism might in a similar way fear a loss of order, but in fact, the result is just the opposite. The greater complexity we encounter is the more complete sort that makes existence vital, and life an option. Such complexity is ordered, deeply, but rather than the order of one thing guaranteeing another, this the order of understanding's richly multidimensional workings.

"The Big Band Theory":
Creative Systems Theory Takes on Existence as a Whole

Some last reflections address an ultimate question that in the end encompasses all of the others: How do we best think about the whole shebang, existence in its entirety? Here CST would not immediately seem terribly pertinent, given that its contribution lies with the human dimension, with who we are and how we understand. But, in fact, just that is what makes it particularly relevant. We can't in the end know for sure what is "out there." Indeed, as philosophers are quick to tell us, we can't even be sure that there is an "out there" to know. But there is a lot we can say about how we think and understanding's evolution.

Addressing existence as a whole necessarily starts with the cognitive lenses through which we make sense of our worlds. CST addresses why through history we have thought not just about ourselves, but also about the physical and the biological, in the specific ways that we have. And of particular importance for these encompassing reflections, it proposes that there is a lot we can say about how understanding today is changing.

Why is it that modern age thinkers saw a clockworks universe, and before that, people in the Middle Ages understood the universe to be ordered by divine principles? And even earlier, why did people think in terms of polytheistic spiritual pantheons, and before that interplaying animistic forces? What people in each period believed reflected underlying changes in how they understood. And today that evolution continues.

CST invites us to reflect on that continuing evolution. I've described how Integrative Meta-perspective replaces modern age mechanistic formulations, in which truth reduced to rationality and simple cause-and-effect relationships, with ways of thinking that are more systemic and also more dynamic. Because Integrative Meta-perspective reflects changes not just in what we think, but in how we think, in the end, it does this for every aspect of existence. And a creative frame provides a simple yet provocative way to make the leap.

For these reflections, it will suffice to keep things simple and talk in terms of the three layers that we tend to reference with everyday thought: there is the inanimate; there is life; and there is this odd addition, conscious life (including ourselves and to lesser degrees other higher life forms). Besides helping us recognize the rich interconnections and often provocative generativities of existence as a whole, Integrative Meta-perspective's more complete vantage, particularly when we add a creative frame, also helps us better appreciate the very different ways the physical, the biological, and the human manifest this generativity—the unique ways each is "creative."

What CST has to say at this largest of big-picture scales is not wholly unique or radically significant in the way that its conclusions are for human systems. I include these additional observations simply because they make for provocative consideration. They also in a further way help us separate the conceptual wheat from the chaff as we look to the future. Just for fun, I like to call the encompassing picture that CST suggests "The Big Band Theory."

"Bridging" Polarities

Drawing on how Integrative Meta-perspective takes us beyond the polarized and polarizing beliefs of times past provides a good first glimpse of how a systemic interpretation may be pertinent. Polarity-related insights in our time have garnered greatest attention with the physical, as the before wholly separate worlds of matter and energy, time and space, and the observer set at arm's length from the observed have given way to a more interconnected picture. But they have been just as significant when it comes to living systems, as we have begun to find ideas that make cut-and-dried distinctions between nature and nurture, mind and body, anatomy and physiology, competition and cooperation, or conscious and unconscious much less useful.

A couple of overarching polarity-related observations prove particularly helpful when it comes to recognizing how our picture of the whole of existence is changing. The first relates to how it has been our tendency in times past to divide existence in its entirety into opposing polar worlds. We've done this in different ways depending on when in history we look. We've also done it in different ways depending on whether our basic inclinations tend more toward the material/scientific or spiritual/religious side of things. In modern times, science has tended to divide existence into animate and inanimate, lumping together ourselves and the creaturely and setting them in contrast to a "dead" world of rocks and rivers. Religion has tended more to set the human species separate, make it in some way "chosen" with dominion over the rest of creation. Note that along with dividing existence into separate worlds, we've tended to elevate the significance of one pole while diminishing, or even denigrating, the other.

Integrative Meta-perspective helps us grasp existence more as a whole. It also helps us better appreciate how the various layers of existence are different, how each manifests as an aspect of that larger picture. Limited to how we commonly think, this dual result can be confusing. But from the vantage of Integrative Meta-perspective, this is exactly what we would expect. Again, we confront the Dilemma of Representation.

Using Neapolitan ice cream as a metaphor helps get beyond the conceptual quandary. Rather than wholly different categories set in polar relationship, we get a reality in which each layer is the same stuff (like ice cream) and at the same time wholly different. What we see in fact stretches the metaphor. Rather than just being different in kind (as with flavors), the various layers reflect distinct levels of organization. But the image provides a good place to start.[9]

---

9   This kind of metaphor stretching should now be familiar. We saw something similar with how the various "crayons" in Integrative Meta-perspective's systemic box represent not just variation, but apples-and-oranges differences.

The second overarching polarity-related observation concerns change and just how it happens. Our standard modern age interpretation views change in terms of simple cause and effect. But we have not always viewed change in that way, and there is no reason to assume that how we have most recently understood change is how we will see change in times ahead.

Each cultural period has had its particular understandings of change. At the most big-picture level, each has had its creation stories, explanations for how what we see around us came to exist. For the Dogan tribe of Mali, it is the tale of how Amma broke the Egg of the World. In the creation story of the ancient Mayans as told in the Popol Vuh, multiple deities came together to bring existence into being. Christianity and Judaism have their Hebrew Genesis. Modern science has its Big Bang. Every cultural period has also had its explanations for what we see day to day—both why things change and why too they are as stable as they often are—from the whims of gods to the gears and pulleys of a mechanistic universe.

A characteristic shared by these very different change pictures points toward the importance of something more, and also just a bit toward where a next step might take us. Each of these past explanations has been dualistic. Each has posited some separate driving impetus, be it in earliest times an animistic force, or with modern, more mechanistic thinking, an action with its equal and opposite reaction. As with other polarity-related beliefs, we might expect change's picture today too to be changing, becoming somehow more systemically conceived.

And that is what we see. Increasingly we find ideas that make change and stability aspects of some larger concept. Dualistic notions—both of the extreme type that posit a separate animating force and of the more mundane sort that juxtapose separate causes and effects—are giving way to more dynamic formulations. And often, "dynamic" refers not just to having more moving parts, but to being somehow generative. The new picture increasingly puts reality itself in motion. Change and the coherence through which we identify something as something become parts of a single larger, "self-organizing" dynamic.

Our times challenge us to leave behind past dualistic assumptions on both counts, with regard to both here-and-now relationships and when it comes to how things change. Put these two polarity-related observations together and we get a first-cut look at existence as a whole as seen through the lens of Integrative Meta-perspective. Cultural Maturity's cognitive reordering helps us better appreciate the complex interconnections and dynamic change processes that mark existence's workings. They also help us better recognize the unique ways that various layers of existence give this more dynamic picture expression. The systems concept of "emergent properties" helps us grasp this result. Emergent properties are characteristics unique to a set of systemic relationships. In the new picture, each layer is defined/separated/joined by an emergent property—in this case, existence (in contrast to nonexistence), life, and the capacity for conscious reflection.

Applying a Creative Frame

A creative frame provides a concise way to capture and give detail to this new picture. In particular, it helps us be more explicit in how we think about both similarities and differences between the physical, the biological, and the human.

Let's start with similarities. Using our Neapolitan ice cream metaphor, instead of ice cream, the "same stuff" becomes creation. I've suggested that today we are understanding each layer in ways that are both more systemic and more generative. I've also observed how dualistic concepts of change are being replaced with thinking that views systems as "self-organizing." Better we might say simply, "creative." In this way of thinking, the different layers of existence become evolving expressions of creative organization.

At the level of the inanimate, I've previously implied this more dynamic/creative picture in noting physics' metaphorical language of black holes, quarks, and quasars. Here we might add the phenomenon of quantum interconnectedness, since it has gotten particular attention of late and its implications are so provocative. Over the years, I've often emphasized the Noble Prize–winning work of thermodynamic chemist and complexity theorist Illya Prigogine because of the important links it provides between the inanimate and the living. Prigogine demonstrated how certain nonliving systems could be shown to self-maintain and self-organize. His work contributed to an increasing consensus among scientists that the emergent property we call life, rather than being a rare, perhaps one-off chance occurrence, may be, if not almost inevitable, certainly more readily achieved than we have before assumed. It may be less likely than we have thought that we are alone in the universe.

Biology's version of today's more change-permeated, systemically interconnected, often mysterious and contradictory picture has deepened and filled out considerably in recent decades. We are better recognizing how creatures of all sorts are more complexly intelligent than we have before assumed. We are also better appreciating how evolution is as much about cooperation as competition, and not just cooperation with one's own kind, but also between species (think of the increasingly recognized role of bacteria in our gut—they keep us healthy, and we in turn keep them nourished and alive). Of particular pertinence for this book's reflections, the pivotal systems question of what it might mean to think about living systems in living terms is more and more being recognized by biologists as not just legitimate, but one that with time must necessarily be answered.

As far as the human, I've pointed toward how we find precursors to the rethinking of how we think that comes with Integrative Metaperspective in modern psychiatry's and psychology's recognition of unconscious forces. The idea of an unconscious directly challenged past assumptions, and with them, the as-if-from-a-balcony, objectivist kind of thinking that had given us the modern clockworks worldview. In an earlier footnote, I described how we can understand the history of twentieth-century psychiatry and psychology as a gradual inquiry into all that necessarily goes into a more complete—and "creative"—picture of human intelligence.

As important as how a creative frame helps us grasp similarities across existence as an entirety, is how it lets us be more specific in delineating what makes different layers of existence unique. We appropriately ask, if the polarized and mythologized distinctions of times past no longer serve us, just what it is that differentiates these emergent realities. I think of it as the amount of creative information each inherently embodies. Each layer is distinguished by a "creative multiplier" (or several creative multipliers working together) that radically increases the rate at which creative reorganization can take place. In the case of life, this is natural selection and the learning/adapting capacities that come with life's workings. In the case of ourselves, the creative multiplier is the option of fresh creation happening with every new "aha" that arises with conscious awareness and our unique toolmaking, idea-making, meaning-making prowess. The innovations that separate the various layers of existence produce leaps in possibility. They qualitatively increase the amount of creation/formativeness each succeeding layer is capable of embodying/manifesting.[10]

In summary, at the biggest of big-picture scales, the picture of existence that results with Integrative Meta-perspective is both more systemically interwoven and more inherently generative than what we have known. In both of these ways, it is more of a whole. The picture that results also helps us more accurately appreciate real differences. It helps us get beyond the mythologizing and polarizing of times past and better appreciate what ultimately makes layers of existence distinct. Add a creative frame and this picture comes alive and places at the forefront the dynamic vitality—and wonder—of existence. The worlds of the physical, the biological, and of more conscious creatures such as ourselves come to reflect emergent levels within a more encompassing and creatively dynamic systemic picture.

Where It All Takes Us and Our Place in the Larger Scheme of Things

This creative interpretation invites conjecture with regard to a related but more specific eternal quandary: our place in the larger scheme of things. We can put the question in science-versus-religion terms. From a scientific viewpoint, we can appropriately ask—as many great thinkers have asked—"Are we but a speck in an essentially purposeless universe, an odd momentary impulse of no real ultimate significance?" Or do we better think of ourselves as God's special children, as most religions through time have somehow seen us? A creative interpretation offers a third option—neither quite so random nor quite so grand, but arguably more intriguing.

Reframed, the question becomes, What is our place and significance in creation?—as creation becomes what "the scheme of things" is ultimately about. A creative interpretation emphasizes that not all creation is the same and proposes that the answer to our question lies in just how this is so. Interpretations of times past have tended either to idealize the human—make us separate and special—or simply lump us together with life

---

10 Note that this way of framing what is different conceptually parallels how I have used the notion of Capacitance when speaking of human systems.

more generally. I've described how Integrative Meta-perspective suggests that it may all be more like Neapolitan ice cream.

Our place in the larger scheme of things? At the least we represent a fascinating bit of creative innovation (with the jury far from in on just how ultimately successful). If we want to feel a bit more special, we could claim ours to be a particularly significant sort of creative innovation. We are the only creature, at least on our particular earth, that is not just consciously aware, but aware of itself as part of something that has evolved and continues to evolve. In an interesting sense, through us, creation, not just as fact but as process, has become conscious of itself.

In a way, this interpretation makes our human achievement even more remarkable. But it also makes it more tenuous, more explicitly "experimental." It is quite possible that exactly that which makes us special—our great creative prowess—will be our undoing. Our time on the planet has been extremely short (compared to, say, the dinosaurs—for us, 300,000 years, with civilization, even in its crudest beginnings, a product of only the most recent 50,000, compared to 180 million years for the dinosaurs). And with growing frequency, modern invention, and human choice more generally, has dangerously two-edged potential consequences.

CST's developmental/evolutionary perspective has critical pertinence to the question of what may transpire in the future. In our time, the human creative "experiment" continues, and in ways that have major implications for its ultimate success. Cultural Maturity describes the possibility—and necessity—of a more aware and more deeply engaged relationship with our creative, toolmaking, meaning-making natures. *Homo sapiens sapiens*—"man the wise"—is perhaps coming to better deserve his self-proclaimed status. If Integrative Meta-perspective accurately describes the fundamental challenge of our time, certainly our continued creative well-being, and perhaps our survival, depends on it.

The Ultimate Significance of a Creative Frame

Does a creative frame, drawing as it does on intelligence's multiplicity and in the process leaving the rationalist/individualist/machine model of understanding that has defined our Modern Age in the past, finally get things right? Do we appropriately conclude that thinking of human experience—and reality as a whole—as "creative" in the Creative Systems Theory sense, represents final truth? The question takes on particular significance with the recognition that if CST is accurate, Integrative Meta-perspective represents not just a needed next chapter in understanding, but what should be the foundation for understanding well into the future.

We must be aware of not falling for the same kind of assumption that made modern age ways of thinking a last word and ideal. What we can comfortably say is that Integrative Meta-perspective and the more dynamic and complete kind of systemic understanding that results offers that we might better address the increasingly nuanced and complex questions that define our time (as the Modern Age's machine model did for the emergent questions of its time). We can also reasonably conclude that these new steps in how we understand bring us a bit closer to getting our minds around all that is involved—as each previous chapter in human understanding appears to have done. How close a creative frame takes us to how things "ultimately" work is a question we have no way to answer.

A New Common Sense

Integrative Meta-perspective is striking in its conceptual spareness. In the sense that it is a single-brushstroke notion, it could not be simpler. And at the same time, the way it alters understanding alters everything. A few quick observations help summarize both how Integrative Meta-perspective stretches usual understanding and the significance of its contribution:

- Integrative Meta-perspective both challenges us to rethink the human story and makes it possible to do so. It highlights the limitations of modern age heroic and romantic worldviews and also more recent postmodern beliefs and invites a new kind of answer to the question of narrative. The concept of Cultural Maturity, a direct product of Integrative Meta-perspective's new vantage, offers a new North Star able to effectively guide us going forward and an antidote to today's Crisis of Purpose.
- Integrative Meta-perspective brings important new emphasis to how deeply we are responsible. By taking us beyond parental notions of cultural truth, it makes us more explicitly responsible not just for our actions, but also for the beliefs on which we base our actions. And by helping us better take everything that needs to be included into account, it offers the possibility of basing our answers on new, more mature kinds of values and ways of understanding. Integrative Meta-perspective's new emphasis on how deeply we are responsible takes particularly pointed expression today in the importance of redefining wealth and progress.
- Integrative Meta-perspective propels us beyond ideological easy answers of all sorts. By more consciously drawing on the

whole of our own cognitive complexity, it helps us leave behind the mythologizings and projections that in times past have protected us from life's easily overwhelming complexities and think in new, more complete ways. It helps us to both better get at the questions that ultimately need to be addressed and better get our minds around more systemically conceived solutions.

Integrative Meta-perspective invites the possibility of more Whole-Person/Whole-System relationships. In doing so, it also challenges us to conceive of identity more systemically. We find this essential expansion in how we relate to others and to ourselves in every part of our lives—from the most private of personal connectings, to the bonds that link leaders and followers of all sorts, to relationships between social groups, from organizations to nation-states.

Integrative Meta-perspective helps us appreciate how questions of all sorts must be understood in relationship to larger change processes. In offering that we might more effectively step back from experience over time, it makes obvious that what is true at one moment is not necessarily true at another. And by drawing on intelligence's multiple aspects, it makes us more generally able to think in ways that take change into account.

Integrative Meta-perspective provides an array of additional new skills and capacities that will be increasingly essential to addressing tasks of all sorts—from a new willingness to acknowledge ultimate limits to the ability to better tolerate uncertainty. Such new capabilities are pertinent both to the realizing of important new possibilities and to avoiding consequences that could result in our demise as a species. They need not be invented or taught. Once we step over Cultural Maturity's threshold, at least their potential comes with the territory.

Finally, Integrative Meta-perspective invites us to develop fundamentally new kinds of ideas. In altering not just what we think, but what it means to think, it makes possible ways of understanding that more effectively honor the fact that we are living, human beings. Throughout these pages, we've glimpsed how Creative Systems Theory offers an example of this new kind of conceptual sophistication. CST illustrates how Integrative Meta-perspective opens the door to a kind of very big-picture, long-term, multidisciplinary thinking that has not before been an option.

A contradiction I described early on should now make more sense. I've observed how while Integrative Meta-perspective fundamentally stretches understanding and requires us to think in more complex ways, at the same time, when we succeed at what Integrative Meta-perspective asks of us, the outcomes tend to seem straightforward—indeed like common sense. Both results follow from the developmental nature of the task. Culturally mature understanding asks more of us. But in the end, it is only about seeing what is in fact the case more fully.

Reflections on themes that run though needed new skills and capacities have helped confirm the ultimately common-sense nature of where Integrative Meta-perspective takes us. We've looked at how, when we get beyond the mythologizing of relationships—whether between nations, between warring political parties, between leaders and their followers, or between lovers—what we discover is simply the ability to better see others for who they actually are. We've also observed how, while nothing is more disturbing to a modern person than confronting an obstacle that may be impossible to transcend, in truth there could not be anything more ordinary and universal than the fact of real limits. In addition, we've examined how the need to rethink basic measures like wealth and progress is in the end about nothing more than asking in more complete ways what in fact matters to us.

But while the outcome with Culturally Maturity's cognitive changes may ultimately be simple and common-sense, at the same time, we can't escape that culturally mature thinking and policy is today still rare. With almost all of the issues I have touched on in this book, for the majority of people the needed greater sophistication of understanding remains decades in the future. The situation is made worse by the frequent intrusion of Transitional Absurdities and how in recent times we have often seen backsliding in our efforts to take on what more is required of us.

Just where does that leave us? I've noted how Integrative Meta-perspective, beyond being in the end straightforward, brings with it an important additional kind of "good news." The changes that make it possible do not need to be created from whole cloth. At least their potential is developmentally built into who we are. Were this not the case, we would certainly be doomed. But possibility is not destiny. Most surely we will now and then stumble and fall on the way to that re-alization, quite possibly in ways with at least short-term cataclysmic consequences. My hope in writing this book is to contribute in some small way to engaging the necessary growing up on which our future depends—and perhaps to doing so with some degree of foresight and elegance.

WORDS OF THANKS

The people who have contributed in important ways through the years to the development of Creative Systems Theory are far too numerous to list here. To them I offer a shared thanks. For this particular volume, I wish to express particular gratitude to Larry Hobbs, Dan Senour, and Lyn Dillman for their support in the conversations that led to its writing. I also wish to thank Kathy Krause and Teresa Piddington for their caring editorial assistance, Les Campbell for his beautiful work designing the book's interior, and Warren Godfrey for his sensitive design of the book's cover.

INDEX

ICD Press is the publishing arm of the Institute for Creative Development. Information about the Institute and other Institute publications can be found on the Institute website www.CreativeSystems.org.

The Institute for Creative Development (ICD) Press
4324 Meridian Ave. N.
Seattle WA 98103
206-526-8562
ICDPressinfo@gmail.com

CPSIA information can be obtained
at www.ICGtesting.com
Printed in the USA
JSHW010942040120
3317JS00006B/90